CRICUT WEDDINGS

Cheers to Love
Signature Cocktail
PICKLES' PUNCH
Wine
PINOT GRIGIO
CHARDONNAY
MERLOT
Beer
IPA
LAGER
STOUT
Spirits
GIN
TEQUILA
VODKA
BOURBON
Soft Drinks
COLA
GINGER ALE
LEMON LIME
SPARKLING WATER

CRICUT WEDDINGS

Chelsea Barton

5

Contents

Introduction

After leaving the classroom art teacher world, I began my wedding industry journey in 2009 as a wedding photographer, which is where I met so many wonderful couples and got to really understand that everyone plans their wedding differently. Not one of my couples had the same wedding: not in theme, budget, style or venue. I loved every single one – each one told the couple's own unique story through their personalized touches. I was honoured to be able to document these stories through my camera, and I still call many of my past couples good friends to this day.

When I had to retire from shooting weddings due to health reasons (later diagnosed as psoriatic arthritis) and entered the publication side of the industry, I put that same heart into building a diverse and inclusive website, where joy-filled moments take centre stage and stylish wedding DIY projects are truly doable for all skill levels. Tidewater and Tulle began as an online wedding resource for couples in Coastal Virginia, a region of the state of Virginia in the United States, but it grew into something far beyond what I ever imagined – and ultimately it became the catalyst that has allowed me to become the wedding DIY expert that I am today.

As years rolled by, Tidewater and Tulle rose to the top of Google search results for 'Cricut wedding ideas' and other wedding DIY keywords. During that time, I partnered with Cricut to design online wedding tutorials and represent the wedding niche at conferences and media events. Meanwhile, my small editorial team of one and I were helping bring local love stories to an international audience through our content. But like all soul-shifting stories are wont to do, it all came tumbling down faster than a champagne tower. I was at a high point of my career when I was crushed by divorce, loss, immigration and health crises – all within a two-year span.

At the start of that shift, I made a bold decision: to save up, sell off nearly everything I owned and take a six-month sabbatical adventure around the United Kingdom with my cat, Miss Pickles Barrington. I wanted to find myself again, connect with friends and do something 'big' – something I never thought possible given the life cards I'd been dealt. And just a few months into that Great British Adventure of mine, I met the affable Mr B in a laid-back seaside town called Brighton and Hove (or 'Hove Actually' to those who are in the know).

When the universe hands you your soulmate who instantly feels like home, you don't ask questions. You do everything you can to be with your person – right in the middle of a world-changing pandemic. So, after finding a flight back to Virginia, getting officially engaged in Bermuda and then applying for a UK fiancée visa to return, I moved to England. And there, at last, I found a safe, soft place to be wholly loved and to rebuild. I had the challenge of rediscovering who I am as an individual beyond my career and to find my purpose in my new home country. Like many times before, I channelled my inner Scorpio to do what I do best: transform the mess into something meaningful through creativity, even when it doesn't fit in a tidy little box.

And so the stars aligned again and brought me into Cricut UK marketing team's orbit after I won one of their social media contests. A year later, I firmly found myself in the local crafting community as a Cricut UK Ambassador, hosting in-store demonstrations and teaching my own artful workshops while letting Tidewater and Tulle breathe quietly alongside in this new chapter.

Well, this is where this book comes from. It's a culmination of almost two decades of a love for love and a personal discovery as I reclaim my worth as a passionate soul who comes alive through creating with words and ideas.

The first half of this book introduces you to everything you need to know about crafting with Cricut through a wedding lens, while the second half features 22 projects, each one designed to be playful, elegant, approachable and effortless. At the same time, I've intentionally kept every project simple enough for you to easily adapt and customize it to reflect your own wedding theme, love story and vision for your perfect day.

Some of these projects will be ones you make straight away, others you'll want to gather your besties to create together, and one or two you might even decide you don't need.

Whatever you decide to do, this book and I are here to guide you with encouragement and joy. Try to start early, stay flexible and celebrate every finished piece – because done is beautiful, and what you're making is being created with love and intention.

And when everything is all said and done, I would love to see what you make if you wish to share. Please tag @tidewatertulle, @cricutweddings and/or @makewithchelsea on Instagram.

WHY CRICUT IS PERFECT FOR WEDDINGS

It was a fated May 2016 email from a wedding blogger friend and founder of Something Turquoise, Jenni Kidder, asking me if I was interested in working with Cricut on a huge wedding DIY campaign that she was helping to coordinate. Of course, I had to say yes. I already knew how transformative a Cricut machine could be for weddings. Cricut had just come out with their first wireless cutting machine called Cricut Explore Air the year prior, and I had my first 'DIY Vintage Driftwood Sailboat Favors' tutorial on Tidewater and Tulle boom in popularity on Google and Pinterest. It was one of those sparkly cosmic signs that this was going to be good, and I knew that the creativity of weddings was exactly what I needed to pursue.

And good it sure has been. Weddings are not what they used to be. When the industry evolved beyond the limited cookie cutter options, it gave way to couples being able to personalize their special days like never before. We're talking diverse wedding dress styles to embrace all shapes and sizes, stationery that went beyond common templates, wedding desserts that just weren't cake, and day-of-wedding traditions being rewritten. And while the wedding world is still constantly evolving with new, different challenges every day, couples are openly encouraged to break 'rules' and plan their weddings to be a reflection of their values and love stories.

Add a Cricut machine to it, and your whole creative world has opened up. We see Cricut wedding inspiration everywhere now, but in 2016, it was still an emerging wedding craft. Traditional wedding crafts at the time focused on silk flower arrangements, painted signage, made-by-hand favours, home-printed stationery and lots of tulle-and-ribbon-bedecked details. It was generally restricted to what supplies were available in the brick-and-mortar shops.

With the global accessibility of online shopping and being interconnected by social media, couples can now get inspired and create nearly anything for their weddings in any style they desire. From welcome signs, paper flowers and wedding favours to shoe art and one-of-a-kind attire, there really are no longer any limits.

Yes, there are many different kinds of cutting machines out there, but you'll discover that my heart is anchored to Cricut and the community that they have built, as it's a beautiful, beginner-friendly environment where everyone is welcome, especially first-time crafters. It was the brand that gave a smaller niche Virginia wedding editor-in-chief a chance to be part of the greater, national wedding DIY conversation. Since then, I've designed and made over 200 different Cricut wedding projects for Tidewater and Tulle, speaking engagements, photo shoots, my own wedding, a pandemic-era wedding sign business with Mr B, other wedding media websites and more.

Between the creative freedom, product quality, a mix of budget price points and its supportive community, it's all the reason behind why I believe Cricut is the perfect gateway into crafting for your wedding, for beginner and experienced crafters alike.

And at the end of the day? DIY is not just practical. It's a creative celebration in itself.

Chelsea

welcome to
MARINA'S
bridal shower

Cricut Machines & Accessories

You can't have a Cricut book without introducing the main characters, so let's meet the cutting machines that can bring your wedding DIY ideas to life. No matter your budget, space or level of crafting confidence, each one is ready to help you craft your own personal wedding story.

CRICUT MACHINES

Even if you're brand new to Cricut, chances are you've spotted a few sleek machines on the shelves of your favourite craft shop and wondered what they do. At the time of writing, there were five different Cricut cutting machines available: the compact Cricut Joy™, the slightly larger Cricut Joy Xtra™, the versatile Cricut Explore™, the powerhouse Cricut Maker™ and the extra-wide format Cricut Venture™. Some machines have numbers after their names; these indicate the model's generation and can be super helpful when researching features or comparing options for your wedding DIY projects.

To get these machines to do what they do best, all Cricut cutting machines must have the free Cricut Design Space™ software app running on a digital device of your choice, such as a smartphone, tablet, laptop or desktop computer (system requirements apply). This flexibility is especially helpful for some crafters like myself, who prefer to design on a larger desktop screen and then use their phone to make cuts on another day because it is more convenient. You'll find your own preferred wedding batch-making process as you learn the ropes!

	Cricut Joy	Cricut Joy Xtra	Cricut Explore Family	Cricut Maker Family
Save the Date Bookmarks			•	•
'I Do Too' Pet Bandana	•	•	•	•
Personalized Ring Box	•	•	•	•
Invitation Jackets			•	•
Envelope Liners		•	•	•
Wedding Shower Vase Sign	•	•	•	•
Favour Stickers		•	•	•
Blossom Dessert Toppers				•
Wedding Team T-Shirts	•	•	•	•
Sunshine Mug	•	•	•	•
Tying the Knot Mini Tote Bags	•	•	•	•
Wedding Welcome Mirror Sign			•	•
Bouquet Ribbon	•	•	•	•
In Loving Memory Heart Patch		•	•	•
Fabric Bar Menu Sign	•	•	•	•
Signature Cocktail Straw Flags	•	•	•	•
Photo Frame Table Numbers	•	•	•	•
Favour Boxes		•	•	•
Floral Place Cards			•	•
Wedding Sneaker Bow Clips	•	•	•	•
Just Married Hats	•	•	•	•

This chart shows which project each machine can make – if you're still in the machine research stage, it may help you decide which one might be the best option for you.

Note

Cricut products such as Design Space and machines evolve over time, so in this book, I have avoided focusing on functions that are likely to change.

Cricut Joy™

Let's kick things off with Cricut Joy. I call this one the 'little cutie' as it's the smallest of the bunch. It makes a great beginner's machine for those who might not have a lot of crafting space or for anyone who would like to see if digital crafting is for them before committing to a more advanced machine. Joy can cut, draw and foil; it's perfect for making small projects, and it's a firm favourite for those who love making greeting cards. When it comes to weddings, it can handle a surprising number of tasks, but you'll need to bear in mind its size limitations and its lack of certain Design Space features such as scoring, and that there is a more limited range of materials it can cut.

You will have all the basics covered with Joy, as it can cut vinyl, heat transfer vinyl, cardstock, paper, window cling and over 50 types of other materials. It is also compatible with Joy-specific Smart Materials™ (see page 40), so where Joy lacks in width, it can more than make up for it in length: it can cut rolls of Smart Vinyl™ and Smart Iron-On™ up to 20ft (6m) long!

To make Joy as compact as possible, the machine is Bluetooth-only, meaning you must always have this option turned on for your device to connect. Because Joy only has one tool clamp, you will need to swap out the blade housing with your pen or foiling tool if you have a multi-operational project. Design Space will prompt you every step of the way when this is needed.

Cricut Joy Xtra™

Joy Xtra is a step up from Joy because it widens its cutting capabilities to A4 and US letter size, making it a great sticker-making machine. However, it's still small and portable, and suitable for those with limited crafting space. Like Joy, it cannot do any scoring in Design Space, but it does get the Print Then Cut upgrade, which is one of my personal favourite features, particularly for multicoloured wedding stickers. In addition to Joy-friendly materials, it can also utilize Print Then Cut materials. When searching for supplies, look for Joy or Joy Xtra family branded packaging. While some materials (such as vinyl or iron-on) can be used across all machines, accessories such as pens must be Joy-specific, as Explore or Maker pens won't fit Joy family machines.

Like Joy, Joy Xtra is Bluetooth-connected and also only has one tool clamp, so you will need to swap the blade housing with your pen or foiling tool when you have a multi-operational project; again, Design Space will prompt you when to do so. It's important to note that while Joy and Joy Xtra share pens and certain machine accessories, they use different cutting mats (see pages 20–21).

cricut joy xtra

Cricut Explore™ Family

Sitting comfortably in the middle of the Cricut line-up is the ever-popular Explore, a favourite among new and seasoned crafters alike. It offers larger project size options and opens the door to a wider variety of materials, making it a solid choice if you're planning to craft for your wedding and beyond the big day. There are multiple machines in the Explore family; all of the projects in this book are compatible with every generation of the machine.

Using a 12 × 12in (30.5 × 30.5cm) or 12 × 24in (30.5 × 61cm) cutting mat (see pages 20–21), Explore gives you the space to create in bulk, which is perfect for tackling place cards, ceremony programmes and other wedding day details with ease. In addition to the other materials mentioned previously, Explore is suitable for cutting Leather (Cricut-branded), wood veneer, felt and over 100 other types of materials.

Cricut Maker™ Family

The queen of the machines, Cricut Maker is the top of the line. It does everything Joy, Joy Xtra and Explore can do, then takes it several steps further. From cutting ultra-thin, delicate materials such as fabric to handling thick, sturdy ones like basswood, Maker is the go-to for crafters who want the most versatility. With its suite of tools (including the rotary blade for fabric lovers, the knife blade for heavy-duty cuts, and special tips for engraving, debossing and more), it's a favourite among quilters, sewists, model makers and serious DIYers alike. Whether you're dreaming up elaborate wedding signage or custom heirloom keepsakes, Maker is built to bring both simple and bold creative visions to life. There are multiple generations in this machine's family, and as mentioned before, all of this book's projects are doable no matter which one you have. Maker's blades and QuickSwap tools are covered on page 26.

Cricut Venture™

It would be remiss of me not to mention the Cricut Venture cutting machine even though I usually don't recommend it for first-time Cricut beginners. Venture has a whole different set-up and orientation to the tabletop cutting machines, but if Maker is the queen, Venture is the super queen and literally the giant of the whole crew. If you're not a beginner crafter or you are making things to sell, then you may wish to consider Venture. It's an incredible wide-format machine, perfect for producing items in bulk and for creating large wedding signage – we're talking cutting up to 25in (63.5cm) wide and 75ft (22.8m) long!

Inkjet Printer

First things first, friends. Cricut machines are not printers, but they can work alongside your home inkjet printer to make beautiful Print Then Cut (PTC) projects such as stickers, printable iron-on photos and other multicoloured label designs. Think of them as a dynamic duo, much like a wedding planner and a florist: your printer produces the vision, and your Cricut cutting machine trims it with perfect accuracy. The PTC operation is compatible with nearly all current Cricut cutting machines except Joy, which lacks the necessary sensors.

You can use any inkjet printer that works with your budget and preference. There isn't one printer recommended over another, but when looking for a printer, I suggest you make sure you're happy with the colour output and ink cartridge prices. As a former wedding photographer, I'm always keen to notice how a printer not just prints out colour images, but also accurate black-and-white photos.

To be able to use both your printer and Cricut cutting machine together, you will need to first calibrate your cutting machine to sync up with your printer. You can find the Machine Calibration option (also currently called Print Then Cut Settings on the mobile app) under your Settings, and you will need to follow all on-screen instructions. This is key to any perfect PTC project.

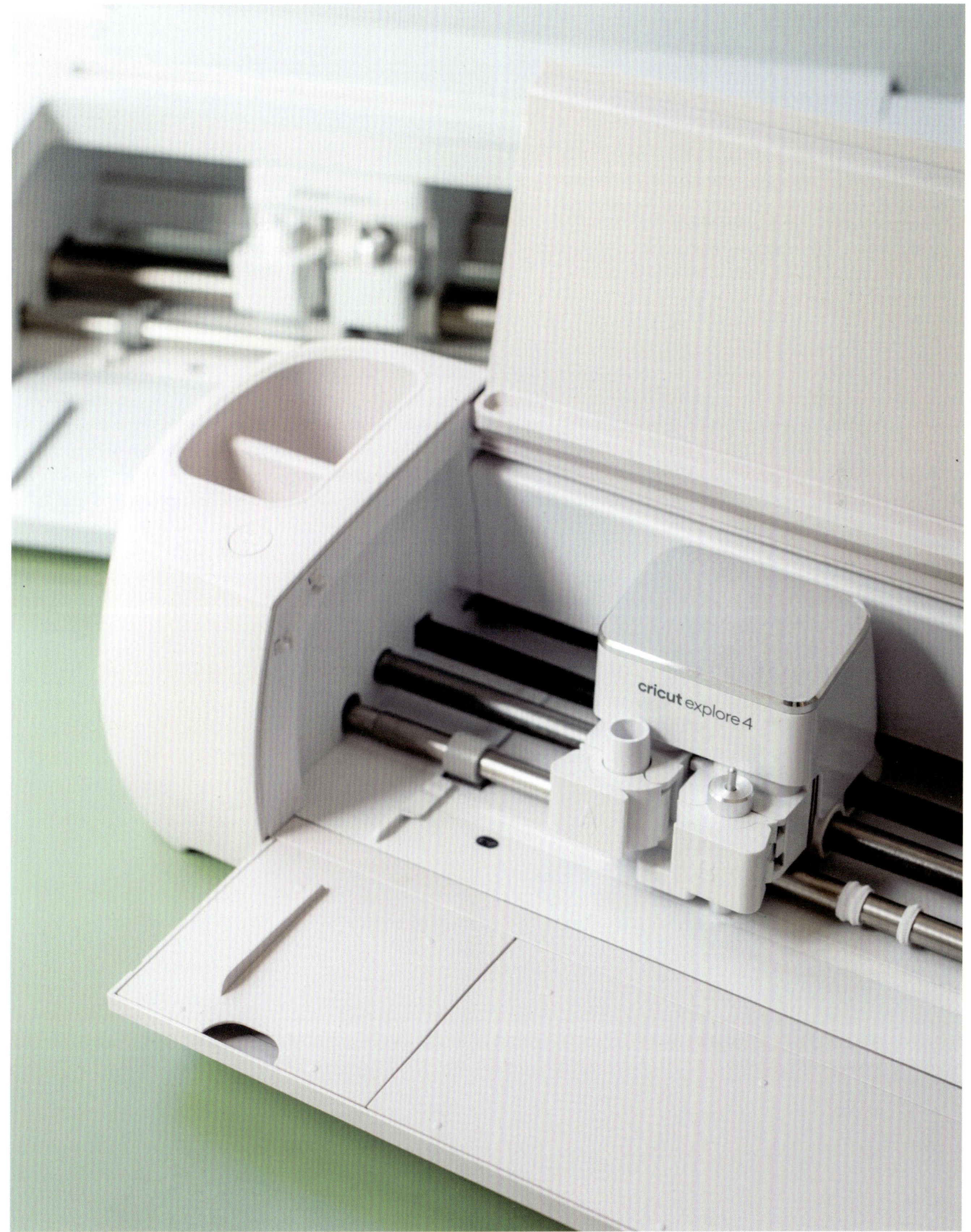
cricut explore 4

HEAT PRESSES

Some wedding projects need more than just a cutting machine; they sometimes need a little heat to work their magic. Whether it's adding heat transfer vinyl to cocktail napkins or creating custom signage on fabric, heat is the secret ingredient behind some stunning DIYs. Cricut offers several heat press options to make this easier: for larger projects, the Cricut EasyPress™ or Cricut Autopress™ may be a better fit than the smaller EasyPress Mini™. And if you don't have a heat press at all, don't worry! A regular household iron will do the trick for most of the projects in this book.

Cricut Heat Guide is the online go-to resource when it comes to all of your projects. It will tell you in an easy-to-understand way what temperature the heat press will need to be and for how long you should press it down. If a material is not listed on this site, you may need to do some additional research online to see what others have done before, or you can do sample tests with spare pieces of material; always start on a low heat setting and press for a short time with any trial runs.

To work in conjunction with the heat presses, there are two types of heat-resistant tape that you may need to secure your material and project blank together: regular (blue in colour) and strong (purple in colour). With most projects, regular will suffice, if needed at all. However, for curved surfaces, such as my Just Married Hats project (see pages 136–139), and for some fabrics with certain textures or chemical treatments, you may need something stronger so your design doesn't shift while being pressed, and that's where strong tape comes in handy. Always test the tape on a discreet part of the fabric before using it.

For most projects that use a heat press, you will also need a heat-resistant mat (see page 22).

Cricut EasyPress™

EasyPress is Cricut's gold-star solution for heat-related projects: it combines the ease of an iron with the precision of a crafter's heat press. It currently comes in three sizes: EasyPress Mini, 9 × 9in (22.5 × 22.5cm) EasyPress, and 12 × 10in (30 × 25cm) EasyPress. While there are a few different generations (discernible by their different colours) of these presses, all the projects in this book will work well with any of them. Cricut EasyPress Mini is perfect for small, detailed or hard-to-reach areas like luggage tags, ribbon ends and wedding shoe decals, while the larger presses shine when tackling big-surface designs like T-shirts, fabric banners and welcome signs. Personally, I have a soft spot for EasyPress Mini. I use it constantly beyond my wedding DIY tutorial design work: it's tiny, versatile, totally adorable and well-priced.

You can, of course, use EasyPress Mini for larger designs; it just will require more time to ensure the heat transfer vinyl has fully adhered to your project. However, I don't recommend using EasyPress Mini for large designs with Infusible Ink™ (see page 38).

In conjunction with Cricut Heat Guide (or the optional Cricut Heat app if using a newer generation EasyPress), you set the temperature and timer. While EasyPress Mini has three heat settings and no timer, the others allow you to set the exact temperature and provide precise timing.

Cricut Autopress™

If Venture is the super queen of the cutting machines, Autopress is its heat press equivalent. I'm candidly biased when it comes to Autopress as I was part of Cricut's online launch campaign in 2022 to showcase how it can be used by the wedding world (I loved it!). If you have the budget and the storage space, Autopress is a brilliant heat press to consider, particularly when bulk making or if you're thinking about making beyond the wedding day for community groups, your small business, families or schools.

I have psoriatic arthritis, and it presents in my dominant hand, so for as much as I make, doing a firm pressure with the regular EasyPress can sometimes be a bit painful and shaky for me – and that shakiness is not ideal with Infusible Ink projects! The Autopress handles the correct pressure every time so you don't have to figure it out. Through a detachable control pod, you tell it which temperature and duration you want, and then you pull down the press's clamshell-like hood so it can do what it does. It pops up automatically when it's finished, creating an effortless press.

This is, of course, a wish-list item and not essential for any of these projects (though it may be essential for those with dexterity challenges or disabilities – and then I can definitely vouch for its ease and necessity!).

Household Iron

A common heat press question is 'Can I use my iron?' The short answer is yes! If your wedding budget doesn't allow for it, there are many projects that you can do without a heat press, and you could adapt the remaining projects to make them suitable for a household iron. However, if you're using an iron, you'll want to steer clear of Infusible Ink projects, and swap out for vinyl or heat transfer vinyl materials instead. Infusible Ink demands very high heat and a steady, zero-movement press that's tough to achieve without a heat press.

The big difference between an iron and a Cricut heat press is that the latter has been intentionally designed to distribute a completely even heat across its plate, which gives you more consistent results, whereas an iron naturally develops some cold spots on its plate. So, if you are batch-making a lot of wedding accessories for your besties, you may end up saving time and money by using a branded heat press. You decide what works best for your situation.

There are a few things to remember if you use an iron. Firstly, most household irons have a steam setting, and it's very important to turn this off before pressing your project. Secondly, when a project calls for a high heat temperature, generally you would use your iron's Cotton or Linen setting. And finally, before you heat up your iron, ensure its plate is clean and without any laundry additives, as this can affect your project's surface. I have first-hand experience of this! Before moving to the UK, I had to rehome my EasyPress because of the transatlantic voltage differences, so all I had at my disposal was our household iron for my and Mr B's wedding projects. My rookie mistake was that I ruined a tote bag because I didn't know that Mr B had recently used a starch spray for a work shirt, which discoloured the bag! But it turned out to be a blessing in disguise – it made me rethink my design, and I switched to using a lovely grey jute tote for our bumblebee welcome bags, which I loved even more!

Cricut Hat Press™

Some folks are hat people, and some aren't. But if you are, then you may wish to consider getting Cricut Hat Press. It's a heat press, but it has a curved surface that helps making hats a breeze. Your project sits on top of a hat pressing form, and then you press! Its heat settings are similar to those of EasyPress Mini.

You'll need the free Cricut Heat Guide app to activate Hat Press the first time you use it. After that, it's optional, but it's a great reference for recommended heat settings and can give you guidance even if your exact material isn't included in the Heat Guide.

You can also use Hat Press to personalize many different things other than hats, such as fabric pumpkins (hello, autumn weddings!), adorable plushies (for your littlest wedding VIPs) and sport balls (for your reception lawn games). Branded weddings never looked so good!

Allergy Warning

Hat Press is not suitable for those with a walnut allergy because the hat pressing form contains walnut shells.

Cricut Mug Press™

I personally call Mug Press a magic trick as it still never fails to inspire awe in me or the people I teach at in-store demonstrations, and because it's such a unique heat press, I've designed the Sunshine Mug project for it (see pages 92–95). However, like any of the other heat presses, consider your budget, craft space and post-wedding crafting goals before you purchase it.

Mug Press is a heat press that creates dishwasher-safe drinking mugs using Infusible Ink (see page 38). While Cricut-branded ceramic mugs have been tested to be food-safe for mouth and lip contact, if you decide to use another brand, look for poly-coated, sublimation-compatible products that the manufacturer has tested and certified that they are safe regarding contact with skin.

When choosing a mug, bear in mind that Mug Press can press straight-walled mugs that are 10–16oz (295–470ml) in size. You might want to consider a mug with a colourful interior or edges for an extra special touch. Personalized, short, stackable mugs are also great for wedding gifts, too!

Mug Press takes a couple of minutes to heat up to its required high temperature. It's about 6 minutes for the actual pressing for one mug, and you need to wait from 10 to 20 minutes once you've removed the mug from the press for it to cool down before you can do your peel-and-reveal magic. It's worth the wait!

Mug Press is used only in conjunction with designs made out of sublimation prints or Cricut's Infusible Ink. If you're using Infusible Ink pens or non-Cricut sublimation prints with your Mug Press, you will need to use butcher paper to help avoid ink bleeding onto the machine. Infusible Ink transfer sheets already have a protective heat-resistant sticky liner, so if you're using them, butcher paper isn't usually needed unless you have a particular piecemeal design that requires additional protection.

One wedding that Tidewater and Tulle published included a couple who did a wedding favour station of thrifted mugs with a 'Take a Mug, Come Visit Us for Coffee Sometime' sign. I loved this thoughtful, upcycled idea! To give this idea a fun Cricut spin, you could throw in different personalized mugs for guests to choose from, like a pet's name, 'World's Okayest Wedding Guest' or a favourite book quote.

MATS

Every great Cricut project starts with the right foundation, literally! Whether you're cutting intricate paper details or pressing a design onto a T-shirt, the type of mat you use can make all the difference. Here, we'll cover the two essential categories of Cricut mats: cutting mats, which hold your materials in place while your Cricut machine works its magic, and heat-resistant mats, which protect your surfaces when using heat presses like EasyPress. Knowing which mats are out there (and when to use them) is key to getting successful makes every time.

Cutting Mats

Cutting mats are designed and sized for each Cricut cutting machine: all you need to do is look at the packaging to confirm compatibility with your machine. Joy and Joy Xtra each have their own cutting mats, while Explore and Maker machines share the same mats because they have the same maximum material width. Joy Xtra has one mat sized at 8.5 × 12in (21.6 × 30.5cm). Joy has two different-sized cutting mats: 4.5 × 6.5in (11.4 × 16.5 cm) and 4.5in × 12in (11.4cm × 30.5cm). The mats for Explore and Maker machines also come in two sizes: 12 × 12in (30.5 × 30.5cm) and 12 × 24in (30.5cm × 61cm).

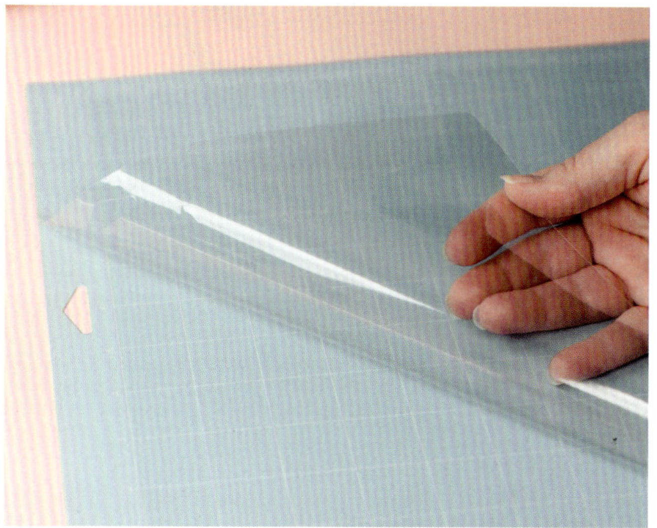

The longer mats for Explore and Maker machines are especially helpful for larger-scale projects such as wedding signage and invitation jackets. Because of their length, they sometimes need support when they're cutting, in which case, use a mat tray extender or move your machine to a long table if it's usually on a shelf. Cutting mats come in different colour-coded tacks to help keep your material stable while operating. There are also Cricut Card Mats for each machine for an easier way to make quick pre-folded greeting cards.

So, what does that all mean and how do you choose which mat to use? As the name suggests, StandardGrip is the overall go-to for most materials. However, I generally use LightGrip mats for most of my projects, as I just prefer the gentler tack more, even for vinyl. But for beginners' guidance, use the following chart on page 21 as a starting point until you are more familiar with the materials you're working with. Cricut's machine mats are designed to be durable, forgiving and replaceable, so you can experiment and make with confidence.

Caring for Your Mats

To get the most life out of your cutting mats, always store them with their clear protective top films when not using, and also consider washing any dirty mats. Simply give your tired mats a light scrub with a dish brush, warm water and washing-up liquid, repeat as needed, and then hang to dry. This should at least get rid of lint, fuzz and any flyaway pet fur (guilty on that one) that come in contact with your mats and refresh their tack. Eventually, cutting mats do need to be replaced when they have completely lost their stickiness or the machine blades have carved too much into them, but keep them going as long as you can!

Quick Reference Guide for Cutting Mats		
LightGrip Machine Mat	Blue	Paper, cardstock and delicate materials needing gentle tack
StandardGrip Machine Mat	Green	Vinyl, HTV and most common materials needing a basic tack
StrongGrip Machine Mat	Purple	Speciality materials such as leather and wood veneer that need a mightier tack
FabricGrip Machine Mat	Pink	All things fabric
Card Mat	Blue	Pre-folded greetings cards

Heat Mats

Mats aren't just for cutting. If you're working with heat-based materials like heat transfer vinyl or Infusible Ink, you'll also need to have a heat-resistant mat on hand. Cricut's version is called an EasyPress mat, and it comes in several sizes to suit different projects, so you'll see a mix throughout this book. You also may notice that my heat mat is always larger than my choice of heat press. This is a good rule to follow to prevent any potential table damage and to give you an even press. These heat mats aren't machine-specific. No matter which heat press and/or cutting machine you use, they all simply provide a safe, even surface for applying heat, helping your designs press cleanly and evenly every time.

If you don't have an EasyPress mat and you're using heat transfer vinyl, you can also use everyday household items to act as a substitute such as a folded fluffy cotton bath towel (that has an even texture and no embellishments) on a sturdy table. However, if you're using Infusible Ink, it's always best to use an EasyPress mat to avoid any unintended ink transfers onto beloved linens.

Cleaning Your Heat Mat

Should your heat mat's surface get dirty, you can wipe it with a damp cloth and air dry. But if it has accidentally met its match with a spilled drink, you'll need to replace it to avoid any residue coming in contact with any future heat projects. This is because it has a bunch of layers on the inside that would have been damaged.

cricut

MACHINE TOOLS & BLADES

When it comes to Cricut crafting, using the right tool for the job is key to getting clean, precise results. There are several types of machine tools and blades available, and some are specific to certain Cricut machines. The good news? You don't have to guess. Once you select your base material setting in Design Space, the app will automatically tell you which tool or blade to use, so you'll always know when you're on the right track for your project. Joy machines share their own tools and blades, likewise so do Explore and Maker machines, and there are some blades that work only with Maker machines.

Fine-Point Blade

The number one blade to cut most materials with precision. If you cut a lot of cardstock for your wedding projects, as you might do with your stationery and favour boxes, you may find your blade dulling over time and it will eventually need replacing. I've found Cricut premium fine-point blades (which are gold in colour) last a bit longer when cutting cardstock.

Foil Transfer Kit

This no-heat-needed tool uses pressure to embellish your projects with beautiful, shiny foiled details. It's wedding perfection! The foil transfer kit has three different tips – fine, medium and bold – for you to choose from. I've personally found the best, most consistent results with the fine tip on smooth, untextured surfaces, as you'll see in my Floral Place Cards project (see pages 128–131).

Pro Tip

To get the most life out of your blades, have one fine-point blade dedicated to paper and one for everything else. You can use a permanent marker to make a little line on the blade's cap to differentiate between the two.

FOR EXPLORE & MAKER FAMILIES

The following blades are suitable for only Explore and Maker family machines.

1. Deep-Point Blade

This black-coloured blade and housing are suitable for Cricut-branded leather, wood veneer and more. It's designed to cut materials thicker than vinyl and heat transfer vinyl.

2. Bonded Fabric Blade

Pretty in pink to match the FabricGrip mat, this blade fitted into its housing will cut bonded materials (or fabric or felt that has been attached to a stabilizing material). While I don't use this particular blade in this book, it's still a good one to know about for your future crafting.

3. Scoring Stylus

This tool will create score lines on your project when placed into Tool Clamp A. Specific to Cricut Maker, the scoring stylus can also be substituted for QuickSwap™ single or double scoring wheel if you have one. Cricut Joy family machines do not currently have the scoring operation available, so scoring will need to be done by hand.

FOR MAKER FAMILY

The rotary and knife blades covered here form the Adaptive Tool System™, while the rest of the tools below are in the QuickSwap tool range. QuickSwap tools all use the same housing, so you only need to swap the tips. This makes using each of these tools a bit more eco-, storage- and budget-friendly, as you only need to buy one housing. It's worth noting that there are blade-only replacement kits for the Adaptive Tool System rotary and knife blades, so you can factor that into your peace of mind and budget.

4. Rotary Blade

For delicate materials and fabrics, the rotary blade is a well-loved one and can be used to cut materials like linen fabric, crepe paper, unbonded felt, heavy leather and more. It's one of my most-used blades, after fine-point.

5. Knife Blade

If you want to cut dense materials up to 0.094in (2.4mm) thick, like basswood and chipboard for wedding chair signage, you'll need this blade. You may also need this for the Honeymoon Luggage Tags project (see pages 140–143), depending on what tooling leather you use.

6. Engraving Tip

A really fun addition for your Cricut collection, the engraving tip will enable you to engrave on metal wedding cake servers, as well as on jewellery for your bridesmaids or on acrylic gift tags for your guests.

7. Debossing Tip

Use the debossing tip to create line art on your wedding stationery. It's stunning as it can help you create a unique, subtle, colourless decoration on your invitation suite! If you don't have a Cricut Maker, you can also use your machine's relevant foil transfer kit (without the foil) as a debossing hack.

8. Perforation Blade

This blade creates broken line cuts on materials, which could make for a thoughtful wedding gift tear-off coupon book or reception entertainment tickets for any children who are in attendance.

9. Wavy Blade

If you want to create a fun edge to certain images or shapes for your bach party or groovy-themed wedding, the wavy blade can give you that aesthetic.

10. Scoring Wheel

If you don't have a scoring stylus, then a scoring wheel can be used instead, and vice versa. Cricut also has a QuickSwap double scoring wheel tool that can be helpful with folding thicker materials like poster board if you wish to explore that option.

1
2
3
4
5
6
7
8
9
10

Tools

Machines may get the spotlight, but it's the tools, adhesives and pens that help transform your projects. Consider this your starter list of crafting essentials – small, but mighty supplies that will quickly become your wedding DIY go-tos.

ADHESIVES

I don't know about you, but I grew up with good ole Elmer's PVA white glue. And back when I was a classroom teacher, glue sticks and that white glue were my everyday go-tos. So, when I started crafting, I had no clue just how many different types of adhesives existed. Spoiler alert: glue is not a one-size-fits-all situation. What works in a classroom isn't always the best choice for delicate paper or textured leather projects, especially when it comes to wedding keepsakes that are meant to last.

To start building your craft supply stash, I recommend getting a go-to dry adhesive, a reliable wet adhesive and a hot glue gun. You might add more as you go, but that trio is a solid foundation to begin with! In the craft world, the key features to look for in an adhesive are: acid-free, permanent bond and quick-drying. This will help keep your mementoes looking like the day you made them. For dry adhesives, I rely on Crafter's Companion™ Glue Tape Pen rollers loaded with the dots cartridge for light paper materials and traditional glue dots for quick clean applications for thicker materials. For wet adhesives, Bearly Art® Precision Craft Glue is my favourite, especially since refilling the little squeezy bottles is kind to my arthritic hands! And let's not forget the ultimate crafting MVP: the hot glue gun. When nothing else will stick, it'll tackle the toughest jobs!

There's no hard-and-fast rule on when to use which one, but for me, it's about the types of paper or other material you're working with and what will make the least mess. For 3D projects such as the Favour Boxes (see pages 124–127), I use craft glue as it offers a strong hold and gives me s§ome wiggle room when assembling. For thin paper such as Envelope Liners (see pages 72–75), I go with the tape roller to avoid warping and to keep things speedy when making multiple copies. For flat mixed media such as Floral Place Cards (see pages 128–131), glue dots are perfect since they adhere well to different surfaces. And for anything tricky – like my Blossom Dessert Toppers (see pages 84–87) which need an ultra-strong, fast-drying bond – hot glue has never let me down.

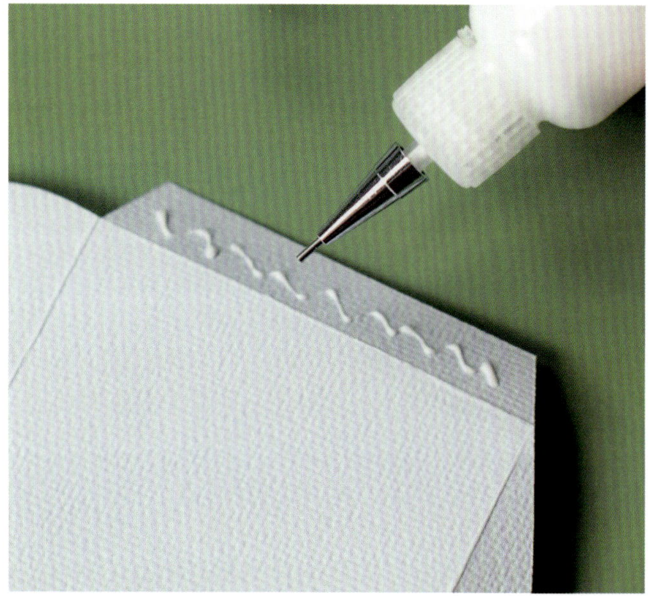

HI-TACK
CE RoHS
HI-TACK

PENS

Cricut pens are a beloved favourite in the crafting world – and for good reason. They make it incredibly easy to add seamless handwritten details, elegant line art and personalized touches to your wedding projects, all with the precision of your cutting machine. Available in a rainbow of colours and a variety of nib sizes, Cricut pens offer something for every aesthetic. Some pen types come in more shades than others, so it's worth exploring your options to find just the right match for your theme. And here's a fun fact: these pens can last for years if stored tip-down (or flat), away from sunlight and tightly capped – which is why you'll often find seasoned crafters with entire collections of pens. For my own projects, I reach for the extra fine point pen again and again, as its delicate lines are perfect for creating that chic, romantic feel that weddings are all about.

It's important to note that Design Space doesn't have a fill function for its Writing operation; it can only draw single lines or an outline. So, if your heart is set on a certain font for your wedding stationery and it isn't a compatible Writing-specific font, you may need to manually colour in your wording or design after it's been drawn with your machine.

Joy and Joy Xtra share their own pens, as do Explore and Maker machines, as they were designed to fit inside each machine's respective tool clamps. (It's also why so many crafters have a collection if they have more than one cutting machine!) Joy family pens say 'Cricut Joy' directly on the pen, and they have a shorter, more rounded pen design, so they're easy to tell apart from Explore/Maker pens. Most Cricut pens have a letter on the bottom cap that indicates what type of pen it is. If a pen has one of these codes, it's listed below after the name and size.

Extra Fine Point Pens (0.3mm/XF)

Perfect for detailed work, elegant writing and intricate designs. These are especially great for addressing your invitation envelopes and all other stationery bits, as you'll see in my pen-related projects! I use these pens the most for wedding stationery projects.

Fine Point Pens (0.4mm/F)

All-round go-to for most paper projects for writing and drawing. These are my favourites for smooth textured paper as they have the most available colour variety, which could be great for favour gift tags or wedding-themed colouring sheets for the kids' table.

Medium Point Metallic Markers (1.0mm/M)

With their chunkier, marker-like nibs, these markers can be lovely for labelling your wedding organization bag tags and boxes. Anything metallic is always wedding-perfect!

Gel Pens (1.0mm/G)

My second favourite because they always give a smooth, consistent line on textured paper. Their colours write vibrantly, making them great for handmade thank you cards.

Glitter Gel Pens (0.8mm/GG)

Just as it says, it's the glitter version of the gel pen with a slightly smaller nib. Who wouldn't want a little sparkle?!

Calligraphy Pens (2.0mm/C)

These pens were designed for decorative writing, so if you love traditional thick lines in your lettering, you may want to try them.

Permanent Markers (1.0mm and 2.5mm)

Extra thick and bold, these types of markers can be used on any surface that you would use any other type of permanent marker. If you're creating directional wedding signage to tell guests where to go, you can have your machine write on adhesive vinyl and then peel, stick and display.

Infusible Ink Pens and Markers (0.4mm/F and 1.0mm/M)

Use these pens and markers for creating designs that 'infuse' into compatible materials for a permanent finish. See page 38 for more details.

Watercolour Markers and Water Brush (1.0mm)

This set of markers and brush is a neat, creative option for those who love the soft and dreamy aesthetic on wedding stationery. Your machine will draw out your design, and then you can use the water brush to get that watercolour look. This works best on watercolour paper.

Washable Fabric Pen (1.0mm/M)

While a little lesser known, this pen is blue upon application, but once water comes in contact, it disappears! This would be perfect for personalizing your own wedding jacket if you learn a few embroidery stitches – have your Cricut machine sketch out your design using this pen onto water-soluble, sticky embroidery paper, and you'll have an instant guide for where to stitch.

cricut joy
Pen 0.4, Sage
Gel Pen 1.0, Something Blue
Stylo Gel 1.0, Quelque Chose de Bleu
Cricut
cricut joy
cricut infusible ink
Cricut
Opaque Gel Pen 1.0 mm, White
Opaque Stylo Gel 1.0 mm, Blanc
0.4 Tip, Armadillo
Pointe 0.4, Tatou
Punta 0.4, Armadillo
Cricut
cricut infusible ink
Gel Pen 1.0, Gray
Cricut
cricut joy
Stylo 0.4, Greige
Cricut
Pointe 0.4, Cactus Rose
Calligraphy 2.0, Gold

HAND TOOLS

Like every DIY project, wedding crafting with your Cricut machine starts with a few essential tools, so here's your shortlist of must-haves (and maybe a few love-to-haves) to get you started.

1. Weeder

If you see something that looks like a dental tool, you've found the weeder! This is needed for your vinyl and heat transfer vinyl projects, as they help remove all of the bits of material that you don't want on your final project. There are a variety of weeder types, so you can choose which one you like best. I prefer the standard hook weeder for certain projects, and the straight piercing weeder for others. When you weed, it's a good practice to always pull away from your design so you can avoid any accidental rips (that was a 'been there, done that' moment for me).

2. Scissors

Any kind will do, but the small Cricut precision scissors are especially great for hand-cutting materials if you're looking for a quality, sharp pair to add to your collection.

3. Scraper

Think dough scraper, but make it crafty. This plastic tool helps to remove leftover materials from your cutting mat and to easily fold score lines on cardstock. Cricut also makes a larger XL scraper; its wide width is great for clearing your mats quickly and folding larger projects.

4. Tweezers

You love them or you hate them when you're a Cricut crafter, but they can actually come in handy when dealing with tiny pieces of paper and for the Blossom Dessert Toppers project (see pages 84–87). Like the weeder, you'll find there are a variety of Cricut tweezers to choose from. I prefer fine (or precision) tweezers myself, but a lot of experienced crafters adore Cricut's basic tweezers, which have a reverse grip design (squeezing the handle opens them and releasing the handle clamps them shut).

5. Spatula

It's like the scraper, but on a long handle. The spatula helps lift thicker, delicate materials (like wood veneer) off your cutting mat, especially from the StrongGrip mat.

6. Brayer

If you're familiar with lino printing, then you'll be familiar with this tool. The brayer is useful for making sure your material is properly adhered to your cutting mat. Human hands are not always ideal, as we have oil and sweat that could transfer to our materials, so it's good to use a brayer, particularly for Infusible Ink projects.

7. Portable Trimmer

Although it's not required to make any of these projects in this book, I use this unsung hero of the Cricut tools to cut down most materials because it helps me cut in a straight line. You can purchase replacement blades when needed, and you can also swap out the blade and place a scoring edge for an additional scoring tool option (so if you have Cricut Joy, this might be a must-have for you!). Look underneath the trimmer, and you'll find convenient storage slots for these blades, too.

8. Rotary Cutter

These essentially are the craft world's pizza cutters, and the Cricut versions come in two different blade sizes: 45mm and 60mm. Rotary cutters are the go-to for cutting fabric (and quite seriously, my craft office's wallpaper!), and they're lovely. While none of these projects require them, I used one to trim the fabric for the Bar Menu (pages 112–115), so you might want one, too, if you go the fabric wedding sign route!

6
1
2
5
4
8
7
3
cricut

Materials

When it comes to wedding crafting with Cricut machines, the material options are almost endless: vinyl, paper, heat transfer vinyl, paper, leather and more. If you're new to the crafting world, all of these choices might feel a little overwhelming at first, but don't worry! This chapter covers the materials you're likely to use for your Cricut crafting, describing what each is best for and how to choose the right ones for your wedding projects.

ADHESIVE VINYL

In digital cutting, you can use removable or permanent vinyl. Both look identical on the surface, and both are made by Cricut and other craft supply brands – and sometimes you won't even notice an application difference between the two, as both have a solid stickiness to them. For Cricut-branded vinyl, once the outer packaging is removed, you will see that the removable vinyl has a grey grid pattern on its backside, and the permanent vinyl has a green grid.

Removable vinyl is meant for creating temporary applications, making it perfect for wedding projects, such as table numbers or signage, where you may wish to reuse or resell the objects after your big day. This kind of vinyl won't leave adhesive marks and it should come off surfaces easily.

In contrast, permanent vinyl is meant for long-lasting projects, particularly surfaces that might come into contact with water or anything that will be outdoors, such as personalized wedding party water bottles or bach pool party accessories. It can leave adhesive residue after removal, but depending on the surface, a little adhesive remover may help to clean it up.

Both are ideal for weddings and have strong adhesive, and sometimes either can be used for a particular project you have in mind, so if you can't find your colour in the type you're looking for, consider if the other type could possibly be a substitute and test it out if you think it could.

Adhesive vinyl comes in all sorts of colours, patterns and finishes. Rolls and sheets of vinyl are made by Cricut and other manufacturers, so you will usually be able to find the perfect colour to match your wedding theme.

Alongside Cricut's premium vinyls, there's also a budget-friendly gem called Value Vinyl – an online-only, Cricut-specific product line that offers high-quality permanent vinyl at a lower price point. I love using it for signage projects because of its translucent backing sheet, which makes lining up large sections of a multi-section design a breeze. Unlike other vinyls, it doesn't have a printed grid on the back, just a plain, satin sheen carrier sheet.

No matter which kind of vinyl you choose to use, once your vinyl design is cut with your Cricut machine, you'll need to use a weeder tool (see page 32) to carefully remove all the excess vinyl you don't want, leaving just your design behind. For example, if you're making a welcome sign for your wedding, you'll peel away everything except the lettering and graphics you want to apply. Now, if you're worrying about how much of a nightmare it would be to try to transfer by hand to those perfectly placed letters from the carrier sheet to your sign without losing their spacing or alignment – then don't panic! That's where transfer tape swoops in for the rescue.

TRANSFER TAPE

There are a few paper-based and clear transfer tape options out there, but to keep things simple, I'll be talking about Cricut's version. Transfer tape is a clear, low-tack, flexible sheet of plastic that has a grey grid pattern to help you align it on top of your design after you've finished weeding it. After a little burnish with a scraper tool, you can then peel off the vinyl's carrier sheet and the design will have transferred from the tape onto your project's surface. Not just a clever name, right? The best part is that transfer tape is almost always reusable, so when you've finished your project, stick it back on its carrier sheet for next time – it's good to keep on reusing it until it can no longer pick up your vinyl properly.

If you're working with glitter or shimmer vinyls, you will need a different kind of transfer tape called StrongGrip, which has a purple grid on it. StrongGrip works in just the same way as regular transfer tape. Since the wedding world is full of sparkly moments, you may find a need for it!

Transfer Tape
Cri

HEAT TRANSFER VINYL

Known in Cricut lingo as 'iron-on vinyl', heat transfer vinyl (HTV) is one of my favourite crafting materials. Its versatility is unmatched. With fabric, wood, cork or even leather, HTV brings a long-lasting, washable finish to your projects. What makes it special is its heat-activated adhesive, which bonds permanently to a surface when pressed with a household iron or heat press. Whether you're personalizing getting-ready robes for your wedding party or adding flair to fabric signage, HTV is a go-to for making extra-special details.

As a small (but important) note, the terms 'iron-on' and 'HTV' are used interchangeably in the craft world, so you may see both on product packaging or in tutorials. Don't allow it to confuse you, as they are categorically the same! But within this book, if you see me reference 'iron-on', it will be a Cricut-specific product (such as Printable Iron-On) because that's what Cricut calls their HTV products. Otherwise, I'll use the term 'HTV' to indicate that any HTV can be used.

Made by Cricut and other craft supply brands, HTV comes in all sorts of colours, patterns, glitters, holographics, colour-changing effects, textures, foils and more. Each type has its own temperature and heat duration requirements, so always check the manufacturer's instructions before starting your project. They also have different instructions on how to remove their backing or carrier sheets after heat pressing. Usually, most Cricut iron-ons are a cold peel (which means they must be cool to the touch before removing the plastic carrier sheet from the design), but always check instructions as some speciality textures may require a warm peel.

Just like the online-only Value Vinyl, Cricut also has a Value Iron-On version that I especially love for batch-making, as it can come in a rainbow of colours at a low price point, which can be a real money saver if you're doing a lot of clothing personalization and need to stick to your wedding budget.

HTV requires the same weeding treatment as adhesive vinyl (see page 34) after your design has been cut. I find weeding HTV much easier than adhesive vinyl, as a lot of it can be pulled away by hand before you use the weeder tool.

The biggest thing to remember? Making sure your design cuts in reverse (also known as Mirror mode) so it comes out the correct way on your project! Thankfully, once you have selected HTV as your base material, Design Space will always prompt or remind you about this before you go to cut.

Storing Vinyl

As you can see in my photos, I use slap bracelets (also known as those nostalgic, slap-around bracelets from the 1990s) to keep my vinyl rolls tidy and together. Over time, tape can leave adhesive residue and rubber bands can leave marks, but the trusty slap bracelet is forever reusable and never destructive. And, well, it's also a bit of silly fun!

CRICUT INFUSIBLE INK™

Infusible Ink is Cricut's take on sublimation – a process that lets you create vibrant, permanent designs that won't wear down over time. It comes in two forms: transfer sheets and pens. Transfer sheets come in pre-printed patterns or solid colours and need to be cut by a Cricut machine. Infusible Ink is very dull in colour before it gets its heat treatment. If the actual product looks faded when taken out of the box, don't worry – just look at its packaging for what it should look like post-heat press!

Infusible Ink transfer sheets are moisture sensitive, so it's good practice to always keep liquid at a distance when working with them, use a brayer (see page 32) to adhere them to your cutting mats and always keep the sheets stored in their original black packaging with the moisture pack inside. When cutting Infusible Ink, I generally also use the StandardGrip cutting mat because the sheets are thicker than other materials and have a tendency to curl.

All boxes of Infusible Ink transfer sheets come with thin, satin sheen, white paper called butcher paper. This is essential for most Infusible Ink projects as it will help protect your project's and your heat press's surfaces. Sometimes you'll wrap it around your mug, sometimes you'll insert it inside your T-shirt. For fabric and Infusible Ink pen projects, you'll always need it. For ceramic or hard surface projects, you may or may not need it. Just look at what isn't covered by the Infusible Ink transfer sheet's heat-resistant plastic backing sheet and decide what may need protecting from the ink.

Infusible Ink pens come in various colours and tip sizes. These are inserted into a Cricut machine to draw on laser copy paper (or any paper that can withstand high heat).

The fun part about the pens is that you can even doodle with them by hand for a more personalized handwritten touch! If you do draw anything yourself, make sure it is in reverse so it presses correctly on your project.

Whether you're using transfer sheets or pens, the rest of the process is the same. Once you've cut or drawn and weeded your design, you'll use a heat press to apply it. The heat turns the ink into a gas, which then fuses directly into the surface of your blank. The result? A beautiful, professional-like design that feels like part of the material itself – perfect for everything from honeymoon T-shirts and wedding party mugs to keepsake wedding welcome bag coasters.

Infusible Ink's limitations are – like any sublimation craft's – that it works best on light-coloured surfaces, and that if you are working with fabric, it needs to be at least 90 per cent polyester to result in accurate, vibrant colours. If you use fabric that has less than 90 per cent polyester or if you use cotton, you'll only get a faded version of your design after heat pressing as the ink just isn't compatible.

Infusible Ink also needs to be pressed with a very high, even heat temperature when it is transferred to your project's surface, so Cricut heat presses are recommended over a household iron. It's imperative that zero movement happens when pressing, or you risk the dreaded 'ghosting' effect where your design looks smudged, so bear that in mind when researching the sizes of available heat presses.

You will also want to craft in a well-ventilated area when pressing Infusible Ink – the process has a very particular odour when the ink goes from a solid to gaseous state. Again, total science magic trick, friends!

infusible ink
Transfer Sheets/Feuilles de Transfert
True Yellow
Vrai Jaune
HEAT ACTIVATED
ACTIVÉ PAR LA CHALEUR
Pen 0.4, Greige
Stylo 0.4, Greige
cricut infusible ink
Pen 0.4, Something Blue
Stylo 0.4, Quelque Chose de Bleu
4
12 in x 12 in
30.5 cm x 30.5 cm
cricut
infusible ink
Transfer Sheets/Feuilles de Transfert
HEAT ACTIVATED
ACTIVÉ PAR LA CHALEUR
Patterns, Watercolor
Modèles, Aquarelle

PRINT THEN CUT MATERIALS

Want to take your personalization to the next level? Bring your everyday inkjet printer into the mix and explore Print Then Cut (PTC) materials, which are really fun options for making multicoloured or photo-based wedding designs. With the exception of Cricut Joy (which doesn't have the needed PTC sensors), all other Cricut machines can work alongside your printer to first print your design and then cut it out with precision.

From basic sticker paper and printable iron-on to temporary tattoo transfer sheets, magnet sheets and waterproof printable vinyl, these materials and more can unlock even more creative possibilities for your celebration. In this book, you'll find two PTC projects using sticker paper (Favour Stickers, pages 80–83) and printable iron-on (In Loving Memory Heart Patch, pages 108–111), but don't let that stop you from getting to know the other materials out there. Custom temporary tattoos for bach parties or wedding favours? Yes, please! (If you're curious, I already have a tutorial for that on Tidewater and Tulle – just search for 'Cricut tattoos' at www.tidewaterandtulle.com.)

And let's not forget a nostalgic favourite that many long-time wedding industry folks will remember: Save the Date magnets. Popular in the early 2000s and always ready for a revival, simply print one of your engagement photos on printable magnet sheets, then cut on any PTC-compatible Cricut machine. I always loved the practicality of never losing a Save the Date when it's on the fridge!

CRICUT SMART MATERIALS™

Smart Materials are fed directly into compatible Cricut machines without a cutting mat, which allows you to create single pieces that are far longer than the length of your cutting mat. This makes them perfect for creating everything from wedding welcome signs to fabric banner menus to paper invitation details. Smart Materials are particularly good for Joy family machines, as they can help you get the most length possible for your project when width is limited. And nothing ever goes to waste! Even when you have leftover Smart Materials that can't be directly inserted into your machine, you can still use your scraps by placing them on a cutting mat to cut as usual.

They are available in a variety of vinyl, HTV, label and cardstock products and for every Cricut machine size, so do some research to see what matches your project vision. Cricut Smart Paper™ Sticker Cardstock is used for my Signature Cocktail Straw Flags (see pages 116–119), as it's my favourite Smart Material and a great gateway into the effortlessness of using Smart Materials.

A vinyl roll holder is a helpful accessory for Smart vinyl materials. It is designed specifically to be used with Explore and Maker-sized Smart Materials, keeping them nice and tidy when cutting. My favourite feature, found on Cricut's branded roll holder, is a built-in trimmer, so you can just swipe, snip and go! If you don't have a roll holder, you can still use Smart Materials, but using a roll holder makes handling longer rolls less awkward and keeps your cuts running smoothly.

Smart Iron-On™
Heat-Transfer Vinyl
Vinyle Thermocollant
Wärmeübertragendes Vinyl
Smart Stencil™
Flexible Stencil Film
Film de Pochoir Flexible
Flexible Schablonenfolie
Smart Iron-On™
Heat-Transfer Vinyl
Vinyle Thermocollant
Wärmeübertragendes Vinyl
Smart Vinyl™
Removable Vinyl
Vinyle Amovible
Vinilo Removible
Matte/Mate/Matt
Metallic/Métallisé/Metalizado
1 Sheet/1 Feuille/1 Hoja
Cricut Explore™3
Cricut Maker™3

CARDSTOCK & PAPER

Paper, paper, paper! Fellow stationery nerds will completely understand the importance of getting the right kind of paper or cardstock for your wedding day vision – I'm as picky as they come about this one! For me, wedding stationery is all about the weight, the finish, the texture and the colour. It's also one of the materials most often used with a Cricut machine, and it has the widest range of cut settings.

You will need to know the weight of your paper for your project because this will affect which Cricut cut setting you should select. Weights can be confusing, especially as different countries measure things differently, but it's very important as your machine needs to know how deep to insert the blade into your material while cutting.

Cricut Design Space does a pretty good job at labelling cut settings clearly, so if you're opting for commonly used paper or cardstock, search for that material's name first. Design Space does allow you to alter cut settings with Less, Default and More pressure as well to allow you to create custom cut settings, but as a beginner, try to stick with the established settings – they are already tried-and-true – until you're more confident with Design Space and are ready to go off-roading in your own crafty style.

For cardstock, Cricut has bubbled down everything to three different cut settings: Light Cardstock, Medium Cardstock and Heavy Cardstock. Try to match these with the labels on your pack of paper. If your cardstock doesn't tell you any information, you will need to do some cut tests before getting started. I recommend testing on the Light Cardstock base material setting first.

If using Cricut-branded cardstock, their regular cardstock is cut on the Medium Cardstock (80lb/216gsm) base material setting, and their Value range cardstock on Light Cardstock (65lb/176gsm). For American Crafts™-branded cardstock (which is the one I use often for my workshops and is globally available), its cut setting is Medium Cardstock (80lb/216gsm).

Cardstock also comes in two types of finishes: smooth and textured. I've used both in this book as both serve different purposes. Textured elevates everyday paper into wedding perfection that makes for lovely favour boxes and invitation jackets, whereas smooth is ideal for crisp writing, or pen or foiling details such as the Save the Date Bookmarks (see pages 56–59) or place cards.

You'll notice that a lot of cardstock – and many other Cricut-compatible materials – comes pre-cut in 12 × 12in (30.5 × 30.5cm) sheets. This size is a scrapbooking standard, so it's widely available, and the materials come in a variety of colours and textures. This size is especially handy if you're using Cricut Explore or Maker, because it fits perfectly on your standard cutting mat; however, Joy and Joy Xtra users will need to trim the materials to size.

SPECIALITY MATERIALS

This book would be kin to my favourite chunky romantasy novels if I went into all of the unique materials that your machine can work with, so I'm sharing some of the ones that are used in this book to give you a glimpse of the possibilities.

One of those is wood veneer – a thin sheet of grained wood that is beautiful for adding warm, organic tones to any project. Cricut make their own, which can be cut with a deep-point blade. Other brands' wood veneers may come with an adhesive backing or not, but they are all available in an array of stained and natural wood colours. Beyond the place cards in this book (see pages 128–131), you can create duotone table numbers, decorate a ring bearer box or even make hanging Reserved signs for your ceremony with this material. It's a personal favourite.

Crepe paper, felt, glitter fabric, chipboard and metallic leather are just a few other speciality materials your Cricut machine can also handle, and each one offers unique textures and finishes that can elevate your wedding projects with a luxurious or playful touch. Whether you're adding soft felt floral elements or shimmering accents on your menu cards, these materials are definitely worth exploring.

Did you know that you can also cut things found in your kitchen? From cereal boxes to baking (parchment) paper, you can really get creative with upcycling everyday items while making lovely wedding things, too. My Blossom Dessert Toppers (pages 84–87) are made out of standard paper coffee basket filters and crepe paper. Who would have thought that paper coffee filters could look so elegant?

So, when you start creating your own projects from scratch, look around online to get inspiration and tips on speciality materials that you can use and then experiment with them yourself. You could be bringing a piece of your home into your wedding day!

Digital Assets & Design Space

Now for the fun, visual side of your projects – the digital assets! These include fonts, images and SVG files, and they're the creative soul of every Cricut project you'll design. Whether you're cutting out elegant lettering for your welcome sign or flowers for 3D favour tags, these digital elements will bring your wedding vision to life, one layer at a time.

IMAGES

Images can be anything. It's a funny way to put it, but you can literally use single-colour graphics, photos, line art and more to create your project. They can be sourced from online or within Cricut Design Space™, or they can be something that you have drawn or designed yourself. When searching for images outside of Design Space (other than SVGs, which are discussed below), PNG files are ideal for flattened images because they are usually created on a transparent background. This helps Design Space to better format your image when it's uploaded because it doesn't need to remove any background elements. But if you're doing a Print Then Cut project like the In Loving Memory Heart Patch (see pages 108–111), then JPG photos can be beautiful additions to your Cricut wedding projects, too.

Design Space's library holds over 1 million images created by Cricut and Cricut Contributing Artists. You can use filters to help you search for what's relevant to you; the filters I use most are Operation Type (cut, draw) and General (free, purchased, bookmarked). Some of the images are free, while others require a Cricut Access subscription, or they can be bought individually. You can also search by an image's unique ID (they all start with #M) should you know it.

SVG FILES

Buckle up because SVG files are why we're here! They are the backbone for all of this book's projects, as well as any other Cricut projects you do beyond the wedding. Scalable vector graphics, aka SVG, files are very popular for cutting and making in the digital crafting world because, as the name suggests, they are scalable to any size without any loss in quality, and they can be layered and they are easy to edit. These files can be purchased online, including from Etsy and Cricut educator websites. They can then be uploaded into Design Space to be personalized if you wish.

There are 22 exclusive SVG files included with your purchase of this book, and you can download them from www.gmcbooks.com/CricutWeddings or from my website (use the QR code and password on page 156). My files come in a ZIP file that you need to extract before you can use the individual files in your projects.

When an SVG file is uploaded into Design Space, all of its layers are grouped together and have Basic Cut as its default operation. If you prefer extra flexibility with moving around your layers or don't want your layers to stay together, click on the layer group and click Ungroup. For some projects, such as the Floral Place Cards (see pages 128–131) and Save the Date Bookmarks (see pages 56–59), you will also need to change certain layers' operation to Draw, Foil, Score, etc.

If you use an SVG that isn't from this book or Design Space, check if it has been tested with a Cricut machine and there is a photo of what the finished project looks like. This is important if the SVG includes script or cursive text with swashes (the pretty flourishes), ligatures (when two letters are combined) or alternate glyphs (like loops or curls). These types of designs can vary depending on how small your project is and what material you're using. While I love the delicate lettering for weddings, sometimes thin lines can give unintended cut results, so consider all the factors first. A good rule of thumb is to look for SVGs that include both a styled preview and a sample cut image so you can compare expectations. Remember: not every pretty SVG is Cricut-friendly.

My heart - is and always
will be - yours

FONTS

You can choose from any of the fonts installed on your computer when you load up Design Space, and there are other free fonts available within the app, too. There are also many more fonts in Design Space you can use if you have Cricut Access, or you can choose to buy them individually.

When choosing a font, consider whether you'll be using it for a Cut, Draw or Foil operation. For Cut operations, choose a font that has well-defined outlines and robust strokes. Draw or Foil operations both use a single line to trace the letters. If you choose a standard (filled) font, the pen or foil tool will only draw or foil the outline, not the inside. To get true single-line writing, look for fonts labelled as 'Writing' in Design Space or 'Monoline' if using another font library.

As well as the type of operation, think about the size of your text – small, intricate fonts may not cut, draw or foil well. Small projects usually work better with fonts with consistently thick lines, whereas larger projects work better with thinner fonts (think about those beautiful scripty wedding fonts!).

Your materials may also affect your font choice. Where vinyl, pens and HTV shine with delicate fonts, cutting these from cardstock isn't always the most successful. Consider your project when designing.

While many fonts will have italic, bold and bold italic styles that you can choose from the Style drop-down menu in Design Space, some will also have a Writing style. Normally, this is used when you're using the Draw operation because it tells your machine to draw a single stroke rather than the outline of the letters.

If you're using a font that you've not used before, or you're using it for a different operation to what you've used it for before, it's always best to do a test cut before getting started to check it will produce the results you're after.

If you want more visual inspiration on what works for cutting, head to www.tidewaterandtulle.com and search 'Cricut fonts', and you'll find some of the Cricut-friendly wedding fonts that I love the most.

Together
is a
beautiful
place to be
MARINA & ALASTAIR

DESIGN SPACE

Cricut Design Space™ is the free app that you need to use with your Cricut machine and it can be installed on your smartphone, tablet, laptop or desktop computer as long as your device meets the minimum system requirements. I'm not going to deep dive into Design Space as this app is constantly evolving; instead, I'm going to cover here the essentials so you can start making your wedding projects straight away.

Within Design Space, there is something called Cricut Access™ – it's the lowercase green 'a' icon you'll often see on images, fonts and ready-made projects. Cricut Access is an optional paid monthly or annual subscription that grants you access to Cricut's massive digital asset library, and it also allows you to use some special features within Design Space. If you've just purchased a new Cricut cutting machine, there is a free trial you can activate to see if it's beneficial to you or not. I do use a few Cricut Access assets and features in this book for convenience, but I also give alternatives that don't require Cricut Access.

1. Create an Account and Calibrate Your Machine

When you open Design Space for the first time or need to register a new machine, you will need to create an account with your email address. You can change this email address at any time, but it will always be how you log into your account. If you haven't registered anything yet, go to Cricut's website and create an account.

If not already prompted, this is also a good time to calibrate your Cricut cutting machine for Print Then Cut projects – you will find this under Settings. You'll need your inkjet printer, a sheet of printer paper and a LightGrip cutting mat.

2. Create a New Project

When you open Design Space, click on New Project (or the green button with a plus sign on the mobile app) to move on to the Blank Canvas screen or the screen for your listed project type. This is your creative workspace. Nothing's final on this screen until you click Make, so go crafty wild!

3. Add Text

Click the Text tool to type out names, dates or other personalization. You can also change the font, resize it and adjust the line and letter spacing.

4. Upload an SVG

On your Canvas, click Upload and follow the on-screen instructions to add an SVG file. You can also upload your own photos or other images here.

5. Duplicate Layers

You can choose to create multiple copies of your project in the Prepare screen (see opposite), but if you want to make tweaks to any copies, or you just want to repeat an element you've created as part of a bigger design, you'll need to do so on the Canvas screen. To do this, select your design's layers and click Duplicate to quickly create copies – there's no need to rebuild from scratch.

6. Align and Space Things Evenly

The Align tool lets you centre text or evenly space out multiple elements in your project. It's especially useful for multilayered designs or large wedding signage – like making sure each section of a seating chart or bar menu is perfectly centred and aligned.

7. Attach to Keep Together

After arranging words and images exactly how you want them, select the relevant layers and click Attach. This tells your Cricut machine to keep everything in the layout you've chosen – whether cutting, drawing, scoring or foiling. For example, if you're making a wedding greeting card with both drawn text and a cut design, Attach keeps the drawing exactly in place within the cut shape. If your project uses separate materials that you'll assemble after cutting (like layered cake toppers), you may not need to use Attach because each layer is designed to be cut independently.

8. Group (and Ungroup) Items

The Group feature allows you to move and resize multiple items together, while Ungroup separates them again. These features keep things tidy as your project gets more complex with multiple layers (like place cards). As SVGs are always uploaded as a group, you may want to ungroup them to make it easier to adjust individual elements.

9. Create Print Then Cut

In order to make stickers or printable iron-on designs, you will need to change your layers' operations from Basic Cut to Print Then Cut. This essentially flattens your image and tells Design Space to communicate with your inkjet printer first so your machine can cut afterwards.

Save the Date Bookmarks

Consider yourself booked for one fabulous celebration! For all my fellow book lovers out there, this save-the-date bookmark project is the perfect start to your wedding DIY crafting because it uses supplies that in all likelihood you have already been gathering for your big day! Your guests will love tucking this one away in their latest read – and you get to share the first look into your wedding aesthetic with them.

Materials & Tools

- Save the date bookmark SVG file (see page 46)
- Cricut fine-point blade and housing
- Cricut scoring stylus
- 0.3mm extra fine-point black pen
- Two 12 × 12in (30.5 × 30.5cm) Cricut LightGrip cutting mats
- 60lb (160gsm) smooth white cardstock for the inserts
- 80lb (216gsm) textured coloured cardstock for the pouches
- 10in (25.4cm) strips of 1in (25mm) wide ribbon
- 5 × 7in (133 × 184mm) envelopes
- Brayer
- Scraper
- Quick-drying craft glue

Compatible Machines

- Cricut Maker family
- Cricut Explore family

Base Material Settings

- Light Cardstock (65lb/176gsm) for the insert
- Medium Cardstock (80lb/216gsm) for the pouch

Size & Quantity

If you intend to use the SVG file at its original size, which is suitable for 5 × 7in (133 × 184mm) envelopes, you can get two pouches out of a 12 × 12in (30.5 × 30.5cm) sheet of textured cardstock, and two inserts out of an A4 or US letter-size sheet of white cardstock.

save the date

1 First, organize all your materials. Next, download the SVG file (see page 46) and upload it into Design Space, then add this SVG to your Canvas screen.

2 To personalize your insert, select Text to create a text box, then choose a font that you like from Design Space or your device; I used Design Space's BFC Fashionable font, which is available through Cricut Access or as a one-off purchase, but choose a font that suits the style of your wedding. Now add your text – I've put the wedding date first, names second and 'formal invitation to follow' last. Move the text box so it sits over your white insert card layer and make any adjustments to the text size, letter spacing, etc. To make your text a visual surprise for the recipient, it will need to sit at about 1.25in (3cm) below the peony detail. Next, with the text layer selected, click on Pen in the Operation drop-down menu.

3 After you have placed your text where you want it, highlight both your text layer and the blank insert card layer, then click Attach. This will tell your machine to draw exactly where you have chosen – this is very important for keeping your design together. If all the layers become attached rather than just the two you selected, undo the Attach command, select Ungroup for all your layers, then select just the text and insert card layers and select Attach. On the layer with a line that looks like a staple, click on the Operation menu and select Score; this layer should then change to a dotted line. Once this is done, click and highlight the score and pouch layers, then click Attach.

4 In Design Space, click Make to take you to the Prepare screen. On the Prepare screen, change the Project Copies to the appropriate number for the size of your SVG and your sheets of cardstock. Place your chosen cardstocks on your cutting mats; use a brayer to ensure they're adhered together if necessary. Ensure the position of the designs on your screen match where the cardstocks are on the cutting mats – you can click and drag the images on the screen or physically move the cardstocks on your cutting mats.

5 When you're happy with everything, press Continue, then follow the on-screen instructions so that the machine cuts and writes your cards.

6 After your machine has finished, carefully separate the cardstocks from the cutting mats. Gently scrape off the leftover bits of card with your scraper tool or fingernails. Repeat steps 4 to 6 as many times as needed to match your guest list count.

7 To assemble your Save the Dates, use your scraper tool to crease the pre-scored lines on your pouch cardstock to give it a good fold. Fold the tabs over and apply a thin line of craft glue to each, then fold the cardstock over and press it down hard on the tabs to form the pouch.

8 Tie a 10in (25cm) strip of ribbon to the top hole. Slide in your insert card, and place it inside an envelope. Now you're ready to send off your Save the Dates bookmarks!

PRO TIP:

Remember, you only need one bookmark for each household at a particular address rather than one for every single guest, so bear that in mind when purchasing your supplies and making. Don't forget to make one for yourself so you can have your own cute bookmark memento, too!

1

4

5

5

6

7

7
save the date

7
11.11.28
MARINA & ALASTAIR
ARE GETTING MARRIED!
FORMAL INVITATION
TO FOLLOW
save the date

8

'I Do Too' Pet Bandana

You can't get married without somehow including your furry friend in the festivities! For those whose wedding venues don't allow pets or for those more reserved pets who much prefer their home turf, you can incorporate them into your engagement session instead with this 'I Do Too' pet bandana. It's the cutest detail that is guaranteed to bring smiles to everyone who sees your photos. The best part? Modelling the bandana purr-fectly is my tiniest angel and little sister to Miss PB – Juniper McIntyre.

Materials & Tools

- Pet bandana SVG file (see page 46)
- Cricut fine-point blade and housing
- Machine-specific Cricut LightGrip or StandardGrip cutting mat: 12 × 12in (30.5 × 30.5cm) for Maker or Explore; 4.5 × 12in (11.4 × 30.5cm) for Joy
- Cricut EasyPress Mini
- Cricut EasyPress heat-resistant mat
- Heat transfer vinyl (HTV)
- Blank cotton or other fabric pet bandana
- Brayer
- Ruler
- Weeder
- Lint roller

Compatible Machines

- Cricut Maker family
- Cricut Explore family
- Cricut Joy Xtra
- Cricut Joy

Base Material Settings

- Everyday Iron-On

i do
too

1 First, organize all your materials. Next, download the SVG file (see page 46) and upload it into Design Space, then add this SVG to your Canvas screen. The SVG file for this project includes two different layers, one with and one without a diamond ring detail. Delete the layer that you won't be using.

2 Using a ruler, measure the area on your pet's bandana where you will want to place the 'I Do Too' image. In Design Space, resize the image accordingly. A cat's bandana might be much smaller than a dog's, so getting the measurements correct now will help you avoid wasting materials later.

3 In Design Space, click Make and follow the on-screen instructions, then on the Prepare screen, turn on Mirror so the text will read correctly on your bandana after pressing. Trim a piece of HTV to be slightly larger than the image and place it shiny side down on your cutting mat; use a brayer to ensure they're adhered together if necessary. Ensure the position of the design on your screen matches where the HTV is on the cutting mat – you can click and drag the image on-screen if it doesn't.

4 When you're happy with everything, press Continue, then follow the on-screen instructions for the design to be cut.

5 Once your machine has finished cutting, carefully remove your HTV material from your cutting mat. Use the weeder tool to remove all the bits of HTV that you do not want on your final bandana – all that should be left is 'I Do Too'.

6 Preheat EasyPress Mini; see Cricut Heat Guide (see page 16) to find the correct setting for your fabric and HTV. While it preheats, place your bandana on your EasyPress mat and use a lint roller to remove any lint or fur from it.

7 Once your heat press has heated up, do a quick preheat of your bandana fabric for 5 seconds with EasyPress Mini to get rid of any wrinkles and to prepare your fabric. Next, place your HTV design shiny side up on top of your bandana and press following the recommended settings.

8 Remove the bandana from the mat to allow it to cool completely. Once the carrier sheet is cool to the touch, slowly peel back to reveal your cutest wedding make yet!

PRO TIP:

Since you know your pet best, choose a bandana blank that keeps them comfy and happy. Bandanas come in tie-on, snap clasp and slide-on-collar styles. Pick the one that will be comfortable and fits your four-legged friend's personality.

4
cricut joy xtra
5
cricut joy xtra
5
6
6
7
i do too
8
too

Personalized Ring Box

Whether you decide to keep your name or change it, who doesn't love the idea of making our special days a bit more special with some personalization? This chic ring box project can be made with your initials, your married initials or a combination in any which way you'd like. This is also a great project for using leftover bits of HTV. Some couples love to keep these memorable boxes at home for their ring storage, some give them to their ring bearers to bring down the aisle during the ceremony and some just love pretty details for their wedding photos. However you make it, make it yours.

Materials & Tools

- Ring box SVG file (see page 46)
- Cricut fine-point blade and housing
- Machine-specific Cricut LightGrip or StandardGrip cutting mat: 12 × 12in (30.5 × 30.5cm) for Maker or Explore; 4.5 × 12in (11.4 × 30.5cm) for Joy
- Cricut EasyPress Mini
- Cricut EasyPress heat-resistant mat
- Heat transfer vinyl (HTV)
- Blank fabric-covered or wood ring box
- Ruler
- Brayer
- Weeder
- Lint roller

Compatible Machines

- Cricut Maker family
- Cricut Explore family
- Cricut Joy Xtra
- Cricut Joy

Base Material Settings

- Everyday Iron-On

W

1 First, organize all your materials. Next, download the SVG file (see page 46) and upload it into Design Space, then add this SVG to your Canvas screen. The SVG file for this project includes the entire alphabet – delete the letter layers you won't be using. I have gone with a timeless, simple vibe with just one letter for mine as my velvet ring box is small.

2 Using a ruler, measure the area on your ring box where you will want to place your preferred letter(s). In Design Space, resize your letter(s) accordingly. If you are using more than one letter, then once you have positioned them to your liking, select them all and choose Attach.

3 In Design Space, click Make and follow the on-screen instructions, then on the Prepare screen, turn on Mirror so the text will read correctly on your ring box after pressing. Trim a piece of HTV so that it is slightly larger than the image and place it shiny side down on your cutting mat; use a brayer to ensure they're adhered together if necessary. Make sure the position of the design on your screen matches where the HTV is on the cutting mat – you can click and drag the image on-screen if they don't.

4 When you're happy with everything, press Continue, then follow the on-screen instructions for the design to be cut.

PRO TIP:

If you want to use a glass or metal ring box, use regular adhesive vinyl for your personalization instead, because HTV isn't a compatible material for those surfaces.

5 Once your machine has finished cutting, carefully separate your cutting mat from the HTV material. Use your weeder tool to remove all the bits of HTV that you do not want on your ring box – all that should be left is your final design.

6 Preheat EasyPress Mini; see Cricut Heat Guide (see page 16) to find the correct setting for your ring box's material and your HTV. If in doubt, start with the lowest heat setting. While it preheats, place your ring box's lid on the EasyPress mat and use a lint roller to remove any lint or hair from it.

7 Once your heat press has heated up, place your HTV design shiny side up on top of your ring box and press according to the recommended settings.

8 Allow to cool completely. Once the carrier sheet is cool to touch, slowly peel back to enjoy your new personalized ring box – it's now ready to store your rings for the ceremony ahead!

Invitation Jackets

With so many gorgeous invitation options out there, you may not wish to or have the time to make your own wedding stationery. But what if you'd still like to add a simple personal touch? The next two projects provide invitation embellishment ideas to elevate any existing stationery that you've already purchased or made. First up is this quick and easy-to-make invitation jacket. Change up your paper colour, closure type and envelope to create a truly customized invitation suite.

Materials & Tools

- Invitation jacket SVG file (see page 46)
- Cricut fine-point blade and housing
- Cricut scoring stylus
- 12 × 24in (30.5 × 61cm) Cricut LightGrip cutting mat
- 80lb (216gsm) textured coloured cardstock
- 5 × 7in (133 × 184mm) envelope
- 28in (71cm) strip of 1in (25mm) wide ribbon
- Brayer
- Scraper
- Quick-drying craft glue
- Glue tape runner (optional)

Compatible Machines

- Cricut Maker family
- Cricut Explore family

Base Material Settings

- Medium Cardstock (80lb/216gsm)

Size & Quantity

If you intend to use the SVG file at its original size, which is suitable for 5 × 7in (133 × 184mm) envelopes, you will need cardstock that is at least 16 × 10in (41 × 25.4cm) in size, which is slightly smaller than A3 or US tabloid/ledger. I used Cricut's extra-large 24 × 28in (61 × 71cm) cardstock sheets and cut them down to this size; you should be able to cut three 16 × 10in (41 × 25.4cm) pieces out of each larger sheet if you cut one piece at 90 degrees to the other two.

Kindly join us for the wedding of
Marina
&
Alastair
Saturday, 12th of April
two o'clock in the afternoon
Richmond

1 First, organize all your materials. Next, download the SVG file (see page 46) and upload it into Design Space, then add this SVG to your Canvas screen.

2 On the Canvas screen, find the layer that looks like a vertical line and a lowercase 'h'. Highlight this layer and update the operation to Score. This layer should then appear with dotted lines. Once this is done, click and highlight the Score and jacket layers, then click Attach.

3 In Design Space, click Make and follow the on-screen instructions to take you to the Prepare screen. Place your chosen cardstock on your cutting mat; use a brayer to ensure they're adhered together if necessary. Ensure the position of the design on your screen matches where the cardstock is on the cutting mat – you can click and drag the image on the screen if they don't.

4 When you're happy with everything, press Continue, then follow the on-screen instructions for the jackets to be cut.

5 After your machine has finished, carefully separate the cardstock from the cutting mat. Gently scrape off the leftover bits of paper with your scraper tool or fingernails. Repeat steps 3 to 5 as many times as needed to match your invitation count.

6 To assemble the jacket, use your scraper tool to crease the pre-scored lines to create a good fold. Fold the tabs over and apply a thin line of craft glue to each, then fold the card over and firmly press down on the tabs to form your jacket's pocket side. Allow to dry.

7 When you're ready, you can use a glue tape runner to adhere your invitation to the main central panel or you can leave it loose. Slide your own information cards into the pocket, then use a piece of ribbon and tie a bow to secure the jacket closed. Place your invitation suite inside its envelope, and you're ready to send with love!

PRO TIP:

Instead of a ribbon, you could use twine or go for a minimalist look with a glue dot underneath the front panel to secure your jacket – choose something that matches your wedding theme.

3
Cricut

4

5

6

6

6

7
Marina
&
Alastair
Details
RSVP

7

Envelope Liners

Another simple way to elevate your wedding stationery is to upgrade your envelopes with their own coordinating patterned or coloured liner. You'll love the ease of this one! This project's SVG is sized for a standard 5 × 7in (133 × 184mm) envelope, so if your envelopes are a different size and the liner doesn't fit, you'll find many other envelope liner templates in Design Space or online that you can use instead.

Materials & Tools

- Envelope liner SVG file (see page 46)
- Cricut fine-point blade and housing
- Machine-specific Cricut LightGrip cutting mat: 12 × 12in (30.5 × 30.5cm) for Maker or Explore
- Patterned scrapbook paper
- 5 × 7in (133 × 184mm) envelope
- Brayer
- Glue tape runner

Compatible Machines

- Cricut Maker family
- Cricut Explore family
- Cricut Joy Xtra

Base Material Settings

- Light Cardstock (65lb/176gsm)

Size & Quantity

If you intend to use the SVG file at its original size, which is suitable for 5 × 7in (133 × 184mm) envelopes, you will need an 8 × 8in (20.3 × 20.3cm) or larger sheet of scrapbook paper for each liner.

1

2

2

1 First, organize all your materials. Next, download the SVG file (see page 46) and upload it into Design Space, then add this SVG to your Canvas screen.

2 Place your scrapbook paper on your cutting mat and use a brayer to ensure they're adhered together if necessary. In Design Space, click Make to take you to the Prepare screen. When you're happy with everything, press Continue, then follow the on-screen instructions for the liners to be cut.

3 After your machine has finished, carefully separate the paper from the cutting mat. Repeat step 2 as many times as needed to match your invitation count.

4 To line the envelopes, first place the liner into your envelope and position it where you would like it. Bend the flap to create a crease on your liner. Fold your envelope liner down and then apply strips of adhesive on the diagonal 'gable' ends on the backside of the liner. Leave the bottom half of the liner without tape to give it some movement when opening and closing. When satisfied, smooth down the liner into its permanent position. Your stationery now has a simple, yet elegant touch!

PRO TIPS:

If your printer is unable to print onto envelopes, you can also use your Cricut machine to address your envelopes for you. It can be a bit of work typing in everyone's addresses into Design Space, but the font consistency is gorgeous.

If your envelopes are smaller than 5 × 7in (133 × 184mm) and you have an Explore or Maker, you can use a Cricut Card Mat (see page 20) to address multiple envelopes at a time.

2

2
cricut explore 4

3
Cricut

4

4

4

4

Wedding Shower Vase Sign

Inspired by my love of overflowing flowers and a good upcycle, this project turns an everyday oversized vase into a charming welcome sign for your bridal or wedding shower. It's especially lovely for floral-themed celebrations and will add an elegant, unexpected twist to your entryway aesthetic. And the best part? After the party's over, just peel off the vinyl and give your vase a second life as stylish home decor or a thoughtful gift for your host.

Materials & Tools

- Vase sign SVG file (see page 46)
- Cricut fine-point blade and housing
- Machine-specific Cricut LightGrip or StandardGrip cutting mat: 12 × 12in (30.5 × 30.5cm) for Maker or Explore; 4.5 × 12in (11.4 × 30.5cm) for Joy
- Cricut Value Vinyl (or adhesive vinyl of your choice)
- Transfer tape
- Extra-large floral vase
- Greaseproof baking (parchment) paper (optional)
- Measuring tape
- Trimmer and/or scissors
- Brayer
- Weeder
- Scraper or XL scraper

Compatible Machines

- Cricut Maker family
- Cricut Explore family
- Cricut Joy Xtra
- Cricut Joy

Base Material Settings

- Value Vinyl (or if you are using a different vinyl, the appropriate setting for it)

welcome to
MARINA'S
bridal shower

1 First, organize all your materials. Wipe your vase with a glass cleaner to ensure all fingerprints and any residue are removed for a good vinyl application. This project has two SVG files with different phrasing options for you to choose from: bridal shower or wedding shower; download the relevant SVG file (see page 46) and upload it into Design Space, then add this SVG to your Canvas screen.

2 Using a measuring tape, measure the area on your vase where you will place your signage wording. In Design Space, resize your numbers accordingly. The SVG file I've designed is simple, giving you room to personalize with extra details like hearts, flowers, your shower date or even an engagement ring icon – whatever suits your vibe!

3 To personalize your design, select Text to create a text box, then choose a font that you like from Design Space or your device; I used Design Space's Beloved font, which is available through Cricut Access or as a one-off purchase, but choose a font that suits the style of your wedding. I recommend a non-cursive font as it'll create visual balance. Add your text – the name(s) of your celebrated bride, groom or soonlywed. Move the text box so it appears where you'd like it to be and make any adjustments to the text size, letter spacing, etc. Once this is done, highlight all the layers, then click Attach to keep things together.

4 In Design Space, click Make to take you to the Prepare screen. Trim your vinyl to size and place it translucent plastic side down on your cutting mat; use a brayer to ensure they're adhered together if necessary. (It can be difficult to see which is the translucent side if using white or a light-coloured Value Vinyl; peel back a small corner – the vinyl side is the brighter or bolder layer.) Ensure the position of the design on your screen matches where the vinyl is on the cutting mat – you can click and drag the image on-screen if it isn't. When you're happy with everything, press Continue, then follow the on-screen instructions for your sign to be cut.

5 After your machine has finished, carefully separate the vinyl from the cutting mat. Use your weeder to remove all the bits of vinyl that you do not want on your sign – all that should be left on the carrier sheet is your text.

6 Trim your transfer tape with scissors so it's slightly larger than your design, then fold down the top section of the backing sheet so only a thin strip of sticky transfer tape is visible. Place it lightly on top of your vinyl, then check and adjust the position of the tape if necessary. Once it is correctly aligned, slowly pull away the backing sheet, allowing the transfer tape to smoothly settle on top of the vinyl. Use your scraper tool to rub the transfer tape so your vinyl sticks to it. Now carefully peel the transfer tape and vinyl off the carrier sheet.

7 Because this is quite a large design, it can be difficult to place a vinyl design perfectly on a rounded vase on the first try – and once vinyl sticks, it's staying there! To get around this, use a well-loved vinyl craft hack: cut a sheet of greaseproof paper so it's slightly larger than your design and lay it on your work surface. Place the sticky side of your vinyl on the greaseproof paper – with the transfer sheet on top. Rub the transfer sheet with your hands or scraper tool over the layers for a light adhesion. This will give you some placement flexibility in the next steps.

8 Wedge some Cricut or kitchen tools underneath your vase to prevent it from moving when applying the vinyl. A brayer and an XL scraper are great for this! Sometimes bubbling occurs when you apply a design to anything round, so to help to minimize this, use scissors to cut small slits (known as relief cuts) on the top and bottom edges of your transfer tape. These will help you bend your transfer tape around the vase without stressing the vinyl.

9 To transfer the vinyl to your vase, first fold down the top edge of the greaseproof paper so just a small strip of the sticky transfer tape is visible, then position it around your vase without applying any pressure. Adjust the position of your design so it's exactly where you want it to be, then slowly peel a bit more of the greaseproof paper down but without exposing any of the vinyl. Check and adjust the position of the transfer paper if necessary.

10 Once you're happy with the placement, slowly pull away the remaining greaseproof paper. As you do so, carefully lay the centre of your transfer tape onto your vase and rub outwards (from the centre to the left and from the centre to the right), rubbing the transfer tape with your hands and your scraper tool to minimize bubbles and wrinkles. Slowly peel back the transfer tape. On the day of the event, fill the vase with your choice of flowers and place it near the entrance of your venue for a showstopper sign centrepiece.

PRO TIP:

If you are using Cricut Joy or Joy Xtra, you may need to cut this design in multiple parts and use Smart Vinyl, where you have an almost unlimited length available to you, especially if you have a very large vase. Research and measure your blank options before doing this project.

Favour Stickers

Stickers can be used for anything as they come in different types of papers and waterproofing laminates, but they are especially great for personalizing wedding event favour bags or pouches. I've chosen basic printable sticker paper and eco-friendly glassine envelopes for this project. The SVG colours are changeable, so you can perfectly match your theme – have fun as love is always in bloom!

Materials & Tools

- Favour stickers SVG file (see page 46)
- Inkjet printer
- Cricut fine-point blade and housing
- Machine-specific Cricut LightGrip cutting mat: 12 × 12in (30.5 × 30.5cm) for Maker or Explore
- A4 or US letter-size Cricut printable sticker paper (or printable sticker paper of your choice)
- Brayer
- Decorative details for the bags such as mini bows (optional)

Compatible Machines

- Cricut Maker family
- Cricut Explore family
- Cricut Joy Xtra

Base Material Settings

- Printable Sticker Paper, White (Green Liner Printing) if using the latest sticker paper (with a green grid on the back)
- Printable Sticker Paper, White (Gray Liner Printing) if using older sticker paper (with a grey grid on the back)
- If using a different printable sticker paper, the appropriate setting for it

Size & Quantity

If you intend to use the SVG file at the size I have used in this project – 1.5 × 1.5in (4 × 4cm) – you will be able to get 24 stickers out of an A4/letter-size sheet of printable sticker paper or 20 stickers from a US letter-size sheet.

love in bloom

1 First, organize all your materials. Next, download the SVG file (see page 46) and upload it into Design Space, then add this SVG to your Canvas screen.

2 Calibrate your Cricut machine with your printer if you haven't done so already, or if you've been prompted to do so by Design Space. This ensures the cutting and printing processes will be in alignment.

3 To change your colours to match your shower theme, click on each layer at a time and update the colour on the toolbar. In Design Space, resize your sticker as appropriate – I changed the size of my stickers to 1.5 × 1.5in (4 × 4cm) to be in proportion to my glassine favour envelopes. Select both layers and click Flatten. This changes everything to the Print Then Cut operation.

4 The next stage will depend on whether you have a Cricut Access subscription. If you do, select Create Sticker and choose between Die Cut (which cuts all the way through the liner) and Kiss Cut (which cuts through sticker paper and leaves the liner intact). Follow the on-screen instructions for your option. I chose no border and Kiss Cut on mine since I'm creating a sticker sheet rather than individual stickers – it means I can just peel and stick straight from the sheet. When you're ready, click Make.

If you don't have a subscription, click on your sticker layer and then select Offset. Choose the distance you would like around your sticker. For a borderless design like mine, change the Distance to 0 and click Apply. A new black-coloured layer will appear in your Layers. Change the colour of this layer to white (or your preferred colour) so your printer doesn't print this in a hue you don't want. Highlight all the layers (including the offset) and click Flatten. When you're ready, click Make. With this method, the default cut is a Die Cut. If you want a Kiss Cut, you may need to experiment with your base material cut settings, so it doesn't cut all the way through. Try the Washi Sheet cut setting as a starting point.

5 On the Prepare screen, change the Project Copies to however many stickers you estimate you'll be able to fit in the printable area, then click Apply. Experiment with the number of copies until the sheet is full. If you would like to move your stickers into different positions, you can click and drag each of them.

6 When you're happy with everything, press Continue, then follow the on-screen instructions. You will be instructed to first insert your sticker paper into your printer; check your printer's manual to ensure you put the sheet in the correct paper feed tray. Add Bleed is an option for all Print Then Cut projects; in everyday jargon, this is when the colour goes a little bit over the cut lines to ensure there is no chance of white paper showing on the edge of the design. I always keep this option on when I'm doing borderless stickers for a crisp look.

7 After the stickers have been printed, place the sheet on your cutting mat; use a brayer to ensure they're adhered together if necessary. Make sure your sticker paper position matches your screen, then continue to follow the on-screen instructions to load your mat into your machine and cut your stickers.

8 When your machine has finished, carefully separate the sticker sheet from the cutting mat. When you're ready to decorate your favour bags, peel and apply the stickers before you fill the bags so there are no lumps and bumps. Add any decorative bows or details to your favours if desired. Now just try to save some of the sweets for the actual party!

PRO TIP:

Are you skipping favours but you still love stickers and want to give your event a personalized touch? Use these in other creative ways instead, such as envelope seals, cupcake toppers (by using two sandwiched on a cocktail stick or toothpick) or menu card embellishments.

1
6
Canon
6
Canon
7
7
cricut joy xtra
8
8
8
love in bloom
8

Blossom Dessert Toppers

What do you get when you take modern technology and marry it with something found in a lot of home kitchens? This dessert toppers project! These adorable little paper flowers are made out of standard paper coffee filters. This delicate material can be cut on a Cricut Maker machine and its associated rotary blade, and it makes for the most romantic blooms from a really unexpected material. The coffee filter's fibres and shape give a beautiful, organic ruffled look once rolled. You can use the toppers to decorate cakes, cupcakes, doughnuts, tarts, pies and so much more. So, grab your hot glue gun, and let's get started!

Materials & Tools

- Blossom topper SVG file (see page 46)
- Cricut rotary blade and drive housing
- Two 12 × 12in (30.5 × 30.5cm) Cricut FabricGrip or LightGrip cutting mats
- White paper basket coffee filters (6in/15.2cm wide when flattened)
- 128–160gsm green German crepe paper
- Scissors
- Scraper
- Brayer
- Tweezers or quilling tool
- Hot glue gun and hot glue sticks
- Cocktail sticks or toothpicks
- Masking tape (optional)

Compatible Machines

- Cricut Maker family

Base Material Settings

- Tissue Paper for the paper coffee filter (set to Less Pressure; change to Default if necessary)
- Heavy Fabrics (like Denim) for heavy crepe paper (set to Less Pressure; change to Default if necessary)

Size & Quantity

If you intend to resize the SVG file as I did, so the flower and leaf group is 5.84in (14.8cm) wide and will fit on a 6in (15.2cm) wide coffee filter, and four will fit on a 12 × 12in (30.5 × 30.5cm) cutting mat, then four leaf shapes will require about 7 × 3in (17.8 × 7.6cm) of crepe paper.

1 First, organize all your materials. Next, download the SVG file and upload it into Design Space, then add this SVG to your Canvas screen.

2 It is likely you'll need to resize the SVG depending on the size of your coffee filters. When resizing, resize the whole group to make sure your backers are proportionate to your flower. Since my coffee filters are 6in (15.2cm) wide when flattened, I resized my flower and leaf group so that the flower was about 5.84in (14.8cm) wide.

3 In Design Space, click Make to take you to the Prepare screen. Arrange your coffee filters on a FabricGrip or LightGrip cutting mat, fitting as many on it as you can. The filters can be close together but not overlapping to ensure each filter is entirely in contact with and adhered to the mat. I could get four 6in (15.2cm) diameter coffee filters on one 12 × 12in (30.5 × 30.5cm) mat. Use your brayer to ensure they're flat. On the Prepare screen, change the Project Copies to however many filters are on the mat. Ensure the positions of the designs on your screen match where the filters are on the cutting mat – click and drag the images on-screen if they don't.

4 Cut a piece of crepe paper slightly larger than the group of leaves and place it on the second cutting mat. Ensure the position of the leaves on your screen matches where the crepe paper is on the cutting mat – you can click and drag the leaves on-screen if they don't. Use your scraper tool to firmly rub the top of the crepe paper in the direction of the grain to keep it in place while cutting. If the crepe paper lifts during your cut, tape down the edges with masking tape; trim off any excess hanging off the mat so it doesn't interfere with the machine's rollers.

5 When you're happy with everything, press Continue, then follow the on-screen instructions for the flowers and leaves to be cut.

6 After your machine has finished, carefully separate your cut shapes from the cutting mats. Repeat steps 3 to 6 until you've cut out all the flowers and leaves you'll need.

7 Using your tweezers, pinch the outer tail end (not the central circle end) of one of the blossoms and carefully roll the blossom towards the centre. Your grip and pull should be delicate and relatively tight, as this will help create the lovely, realistic centre of your flower when it loosens up at the end. You can experiment with what floral style you like best. Once completely rolled, remove the blossom from your tweezers and allow its outer petals to unravel a bit to create a floral shape you like.

8 When you're satisfied with the look, heat up your hot glue gun and add a generous dollop of hot glue on the back of your rolled blossom, then fold the central circle end over the glue to finish the blossom.

9 Reheat your glue gun if necessary, then put another small dollop of hot glue on the back of the blossom. Before it hardens, quickly place a cocktail stick or toothpick on top of the glue and apply another dot of glue on top of the stick, then fix your leaf backer in place. This tidies up your blossom and covers up your stick end. Trim off any stray hot glue threads.

10 To give your flower a more organic look, use an extra cocktail stick to roll the edges of your petals to create a soft, rounded edge, and use the tip of the stick to fix or loosen any accidental finger smooshes on the central petals. Coffee filter paper is very forgiving! Store your blossom toppers in a protective box until the wedding-shower day comes around.

PRO TIPS:

If you want a more colourful blossom, experiment with liquid food dye or natural plant dyes to colour your coffee filters. Be sure your filters are completely dry before attempting to cut on a machine. For a more classic paper flower approach, this project can be done with cardstock using non-Maker machines.

I found most success selecting Less Pressure for both base material settings. However, it will depend on your materials, mat and blade, and you may need to use the Default setting. As your rotary blade makes curved turns while cutting, it can dig into your cutting mat, so finding the right pressure can help to minimize this. I keep a dedicated cutting mat for my crepe paper projects for this very reason. Your mat will still be usable until it loses its stickiness!

1
3
4
5
6
7
7
8
9
HI-TACK
Cricut
cricut maker 3

Wedding Team T-Shirts

Time to rally the wedding crew! Whether you're planning a wild bach bash or a cosy pre-wedding hangout, bringing your favourite people together calls for something fun and memorable. Enter: the classic matching T-shirts (or another clothing item of your choice). It's a tried-and-true wedding DIY project and a firm crowd-pleaser, especially when you can personalize them with inside jokes, wedding hashtags or each person's role on the big day. You can't get married until you've customized a T-shirt at least once on your crafty journey! So, turn up the 'crafternoon' tunes, and let the good times (and Infusible Ink) roll!

Materials & Tools

- Team shirts SVG file (see page 46)
- Cricut fine-point blade and housing
- Machine-specific Cricut StandardGrip cutting mat: 12 × 12in (30.5 × 30.5cm) for Maker or Explore; 4.5 × 12in (11.4 × 30.5cm) for Joy
- Cricut EasyPress Mini, Cricut EasyPress or Cricut Autopress
- Cricut EasyPress Mat (if not using the Autopress)
- Cricut Infusible Ink transfer sheet, in Patterns Watercolour
- Butcher paper (included with the Infusible Ink transfer sheet)
- 100% polyester T-shirts or Cricut T-shirt blanks
- A list of your VIPs with their team names and T-shirt sizes
- Measuring tape
- Trimmer or scissors
- Weeder
- Brayer
- Lint roller

Compatible Machines

- Cricut Maker family
- Cricut Explore family
- Cricut Joy Xtra
- Cricut Joy

Base Material Settings

- Infusible Ink Transfer Sheet

Size & Quantity

The amount of Infusible Ink you need will depend on the size of your designs and how many you want to make, but as an approximate guide, you can fit 8 Team Wedding images sized at 7in (17.8cm) wide on a single 12 × 12in (30.5 × 30.5cm) sheet.

team groom
The bride
team wedding

1 First, organize all your materials. Have a list of everyone's name, T-shirt size and chosen team so you have everything to hand. Next, download the SVG file (see page 46) and upload it into Design Space, then add this SVG to your Canvas screen. The SVG file contains multiple team names for you to choose from – once added to your Canvas, delete any layers that aren't relevant to your project, and then duplicate each layer as needed.

2 Using a measuring tape, measure the area where you want to place your design on each T-shirt. Since my tees are V-necks, I placed each design about 2.5in (6.4cm) below the collar, but do whatever looks great to you! Since your VIPs are likely to have different T-shirt sizes, adjust the dimensions of the team names for each individual to look balanced and proportionate – a design that looks perfect on a small T-shirt might get lost on a larger top. For example, I adjusted my designs to 5.5in (14cm), 6in (15.2cm) and 7in (17.8cm) wide for my small, medium and 2XL T-shirts, respectively. If you wish to customize the design, add text boxes to your Canvas and get creative! If you add anything new, remember to select the text box and relevant team name layer and choose Attach when you're done.

3 In Design Space, click Make, then on the Prepare screen, turn on Mirror so the team names will read correctly on your T-shirts after pressing. Trim your Infusible Ink sheet if needed so it is slightly larger than all the team names, then place it colour side up on your cutting mat. Use a brayer to help keep moisture off the sheets, taking care not to touch the sheets too much with your fingers. On the Prepare screen, ensure the position of the designs on your screen matches the position of the transfer sheet on the mat – click and drag the images on-screen if they don't.

4 When you're happy with everything, press Continue, then follow the on-screen instructions for the team names to be cut.

5 After your machine has done its job, carefully separate the Infusible Ink sheet from the cutting mat. Use your weeder to remove all the Infusible Ink material that you do not want on your shirts – all that should be left on your carrier sheet are your words. Using scissors, separate each team name and temporarily set them on their appropriate T-shirt for pressing.

6 Preheat your Autopress or EasyPress – use the Cricut Heat Guide (see page 16) to choose the correct setting for your fabric. While your machine preheats, use a lint roller to remove any lint or hair from the T-shirts. Once your heat press is ready, place your shirt on your Autopress or EasyPress mat and give it a 5-second preheat with the Autopress or a quick iron with the EasyPress.

7 Place one of your designs colour side down on the appropriate T-shirt in the position you chose in step 2. To protect your T-shirt and heat press, place a sheet of butcher paper inside the shirt underneath the design, and for good measure, place another sheet of butcher paper on the outside of the shirt on top of the design.

8 Once your Autopress has heated up, lower the hood and let it do its magic – it will pop up automatically when it is finished. If you're using an EasyPress, then press it down according to the recommended settings. Everything is very hot, so remove the shirt carefully from the mat to allow it to cool completely. Once the carrier sheet is cool to the touch, slowly peel back to reveal your personalized apparel. Repeat steps 2 to 8 for all of your T-shirts, and get ready for the most fun group photos later on!

PRO TIPS:

This project's SVG is basic text, but you can go beyond! Add your VIPs' names, the year, the destination location or even a symbol or image to represent your theme. Want to go beyond Cricut materials? Get some fabric paints for everyone to decorate their own T-shirts. Whether you're a minimalist or maximalist, ensure it reflects your group's vibe.

Want a different look? You can use HTV or printable iron-ons for this project if you prefer.

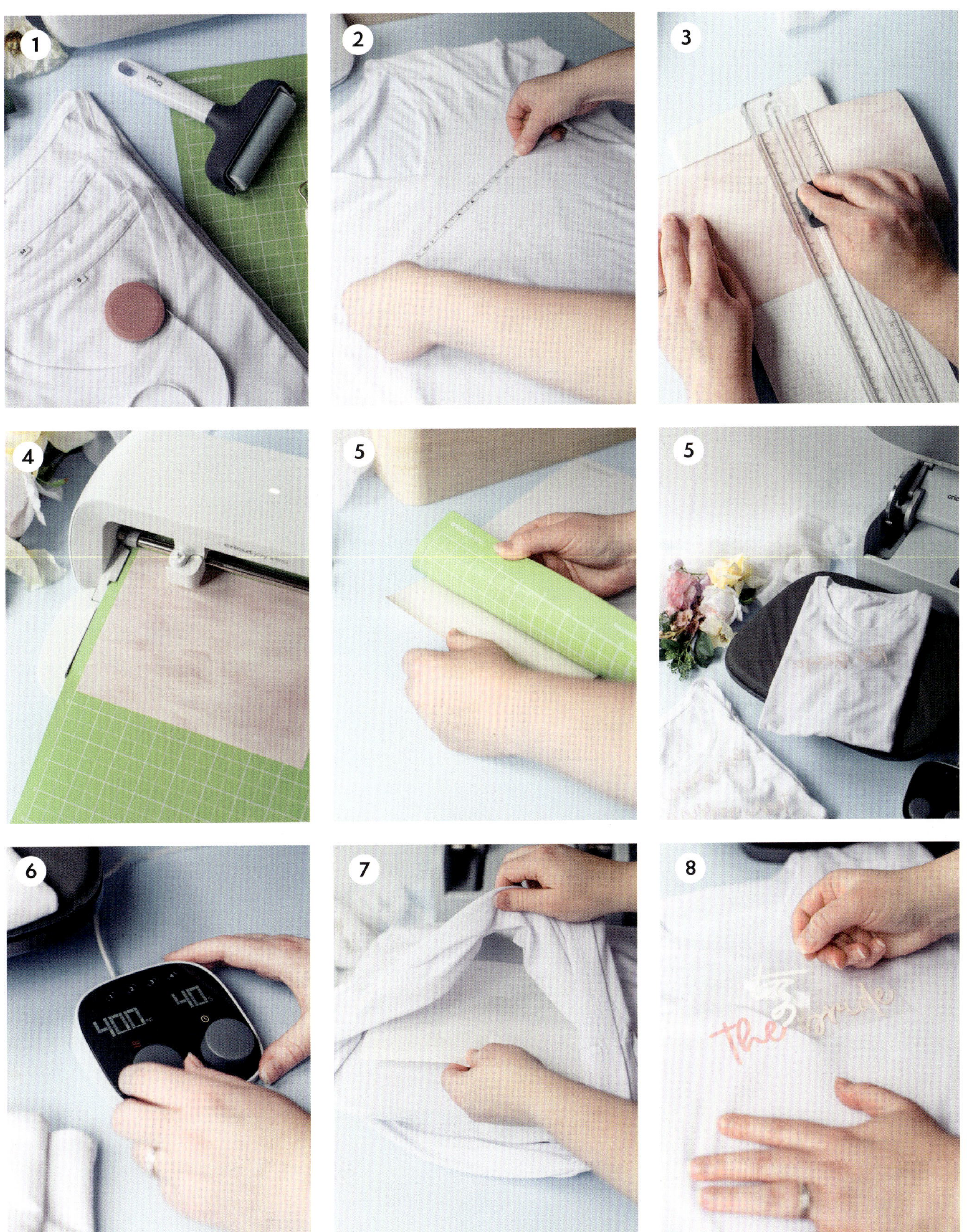
1
2
3
4
5
5
6
400
40
7
8
The bride

Sunshine Mug

Once upon a time, I wasn't a hot beverage person. But since moving to England, I've slowly embraced the cuppa (with lots of milk and one small spoonful of sugar, please). It was inevitable being in such close proximity to an Englishman and his cherished kettle. So, as a homage to my new home country and personal mantra to 'be like sunshine', I've designed this cheerful project for any pre-wedding morning celebration. The SVG features different phrases for the brides and soonlyweds out there who, like me, love sunshine vibes and making memories, and the mug serves as a reminder that it's a good day to have a good day.

Materials & Tools

- Sunshine mug SVG file (see page 46)
- Cricut fine-point blade and housing
- Machine-specific Cricut StandardGrip cutting mat: 12 × 12in (30.5 × 30.5cm) for Maker or Explore; 4.5 × 12in (11.4 × 30.5cm) for Joy
- Cricut Mug Press
- Cricut EasyPress heat-resistant mat or bath towel
- Cricut Infusible Ink transfer sheet, in True Yellow
- Cricut 15oz (425ml) beveled ceramic mug blank, in Miami
- Heat-resistant tape
- Trimmer or scissors
- Weeder
- Brayer
- Lint roller

Compatible Machines

- Cricut Maker family
- Cricut Explore family
- Cricut Joy Xtra
- Cricut Joy

Base Material Settings

- Infusible Ink Transfer Sheet

Bride
AND
SHINE
cricut

1 First, organize all your materials. This project has two different SVG files (see page 46) – choose the one that is relevant, download the file and upload it into Design Space, then add this SVG to your Canvas screen. Ungroup all the layers, then delete any that you don't need. To help your design fit your mug, you will need to use a free Design Space mug template by clicking on Images, then typing #M2B92B531 in the search box. Add the template to your Canvas, then right-click 'Send to Back' (or from your Layers list, click and drag the layer to the bottom) so that you can see your design on top of the template. If your mug is a different shape or size, search in the Images tab for the appropriate size and style, such as '12oz straight edge mug template'. The basic templates are free and don't need to be resized. The template has two layers: the grey rectangle shows the area you can work in without getting too close to the handle, while the other layer is the die-cut outline of your template that will wrap perfectly around your mug.

2 In Design Space, arrange and resize the sun shapes, sunbeams and your chosen wording to create your design, then place them on the mug template within the grey rectangle. Now highlight all the layers and select Attach. If your layers turn black, don't worry – they're all still there! To see them, select the solid-colour rectangular layer, which was grey but will turn to black, and change its colour to something else.

3 In Design Space, click Make, then on the Prepare screen, turn on Mirror so the design will read the right way round after pressing. Trim the Infusible Ink transfer sheet so it's slightly larger than your design and place it colour side up on your cutting mat. Use a brayer to help keep moisture off the sheets, taking care to not touch the sheet too much with your fingers. Ensure the Infusible Ink on the mat and the design on-screen are in the same position – click and drag the image on-screen if they aren't.

4 When you're happy with everything, press Continue, then follow the on-screen instructions for your mug design to be cut. The neat thing about this project is that, if you're making only one mug, you can choose to either keep the yellow background and remove the lettering, sun shapes and sunbeams, or keep the details and remove the background. If you're making two mugs, you can use all the details you don't use on the first mug to create the reverse design on the second. Whichever approach you choose, carefully separate the Infusible Ink sheet from the cutting mat, then use your weeder to remove all the Infusible Ink material that you do not want on your mug. If you'll be making a second mug with these details, set them aside for now.

5 Preheat your Mug Press – it will take a few minutes to reach the required temperature. To reduce the risk of the Infusible Ink repelling, buff out any fingerprints or smudges with a cloth and follow up with a lint roller if required. Next, carefully place the tab at one end of the transfer sheet under the handle of your mug, then slowly wrap the sheet all the way round. To minimize ghosting due to any slight movement, secure the transfer sheet in place using heat-resistant tape on all four edges of the transfer sheet.

6 Once your Mug Press has heated up, place your mug inside it and use the top lever to clamp down the press. Wait until it beeps again to say it's done, then lift up the lever to remove your mug from the press and place it on a heat-resistant mat or a folded bath towel to cool down. Once the mug is cool enough to touch, peel off the tape and transfer sheet. Your mug is now ready to fill with tea, coffee or your favourite hot drink!

7 If you're making a second mug from the details of Infusible Ink that you didn't use for the first mug, stick them onto your mug using strips of heat-resistant tape. Ensure each detail is fully covered by the tape to prevent the design from moving or any of the paper backing being exposed. Wrap some butcher paper around the mug before placing it into the Mug Press so there's no risk of the ink bleeding onto your machine.

PRO TIP:

No Mug Press? No problem! You can also make this project using permanent adhesive vinyl on a ceramic mug. Just ensure you allow the vinyl to cure for at least 72 hours before using or washing it. One important note: unlike Infusible Ink, vinyl isn't microwave safe, so always heat your drink before pouring it into your mug, and stick to gentle hand washing to keep your design looking its best.

1
cricut
4
cricut

3

3

4
cricut joy

4

6
cricut

6

Tying the Knot Mini Tote Bags

Practical, pretty and perfect for just about anything, tote bags are a staple in most everyone's lives. These little reusable bags are ideal for personalizing and filling with your VIPs' favourite things. Think sweet treats, cute drink tumblers or local goodies to celebrate your time together. For this project, I've taken an economical approach by reusing the same rolls of Smart Iron-On from my Fabric Bar Menu Sign (see pages 112–115) and Just Married Hats (pages 136–139) projects. Since these rolls have been trimmed down, and I'm using Joy Xtra, you'll notice that I've placed the Smart Iron-On material on a cutting mat to make sure nothing goes to waste.

Materials & Tools

- Mini tote bag SVG file (see page 46)
- Cricut fine-point blade and housing
- Cricut roll holder (optional; for Maker or Explorer only)
- Two machine-specific Cricut LightGrip or StandardGrip cutting mats (if not using full-size sheets of Smart Iron-On): 12 × 12in (30.5 × 30.5cm) for Maker or Explore; 4.5 × 12in (11.4 × 30.5cm) for Joy
- Cricut EasyPress Mini or Cricut EasyPress
- Cricut EasyPress heat-resistant mat
- Cricut Smart Iron-On, in Gold, or regular heat transfer vinyl (HTV)
- Cricut Smart Iron-On, in White, or regular heat transfer vinyl (HTV)
- Cotton canvas mini tote bags
- Measuring tape or ruler
- Trimmer and/or scissors
- Weeder
- Lint roller

Compatible Machines

- Cricut Maker family
- Cricut Explore family
- Cricut Joy Xtra
- Cricut Joy

Base Material Settings

- Smart Iron-On Matless Heat Transfer Vinyl (or if you are using a different HTV, the appropriate setting for it)

Size & Quantity

For the design that has a smaller bow with the wording stacked above it, the bow and wording are around the same size and you will need the same amount of the two Smart Iron-On colours. If you use the second design that has a larger bow and the wording below it, you can calculate how much you might need by experimenting with the number of Project Copies on the Prepare screen to see how many of each will fit on the Smart-Iron roll(s) you will be using.

tying the knot

1 First, organize all your materials. Next, download the SVG file (see page 46) and upload it into Design Space, then add this SVG to your Canvas screen. This project's SVG file includes two different designs, so choose the one that best fits your style and the size and shape of your tote bags.

2 Using a measuring tape or ruler, measure the area on your bag where you will place your design. In Design Space, resize your design accordingly. Highlight both layers and select Attach.

3 In Design Space, click Make to take you to the Prepare screen. On the Prepare screen, change the Project Copies to as many as you need, then select Mirror as your design should be cut in reverse. If you are using normal HTV or Smart Iron-On rolls aren't their original width, trim your materials so they're a little larger than the text and the bow respectively, then place them shiny side down on your cutting mats. On the Prepare screen, ensure the positions of the designs on your screen match the positions of your materials on the mats – click and drag the images on-screen if they don't.

4 When you're happy with everything, press Continue, then follow the on-screen instructions. It will now prompt you to feed your Smart Iron-On shiny side down directly into your cutting machine, and after the first one is finished, it will then prompt you for the second colour or cutting mat.

5 After your machine has done its job, carefully separate the material from the cutting mats if you're using them. Use your weeder to remove all of the Smart Iron-On or HTV from the carrier sheets that you do not want on your bags – all that should be left on the carrier sheets are the designs. Using scissors, cut the carrier sheets into individual bows and text. Repeat steps 3 to 5 until you've cut as many designs as you need.

6 Preheat your choice of EasyPress – use the Cricut Heat Guide (see page 16) to choose the correct setting for your fabric and HTV or Smart Iron-On type. While your machine preheats, use a lint roller to remove any lint from your tote bags. Place one of the bags on your heat-resistant mat and give it a 5-second pre-heat with your EasyPress.

7 The next stage is to position the bow and wording on the bag, shiny side up. Because you have two different colours and you will be heat pressing in one single press, you may need to do a bit of careful trimming. First, place the bow on the bag. Next, lay out the wording, ensuring that all the HTV or Smart Iron-On is on the bag and not the bow's carrier sheet. You may need to trim your carrier sheets so the wording can snuggle inside the ribbon's ends without any overlap.

8 Once your heat press has heated up, place it on top of the design and press the Go button; your EasyPress will tell you when it's finished. If you are using EasyPress Mini, there is no Go button, so just press and count your seconds. Afterwards, remove the bag from the mat to allow it to cool completely. Repeat steps 7 to 8 for the remaining bags. Once the carrier sheets are cool to the touch, slowly peel back to remove them.

PRO TIPS:

Use this project's SVG to make all of your bach party apparel! From sleep shirts to bathing suits to sleep masks, memorable events always have a consistent design throughout the details.

Each design uses two different colours, but if you would like to use only one, then just change the colours of your layers to a single colour in the Canvas screen, and Design Space will know to treat them the same when cutting.

1
3
4
5
5
cricut
6
7
7
8
cricut

Wedding Welcome Mirror Sign

Mirrors have earned their place as a wedding decor staple, effortlessly blending beauty and versatility across all kinds of wedding styles. Whether vintage, modern or whimsical, they come in endless shapes and sizes. With just a bit of personalization, a mirror sign can transform an ordinary corner into a stylish statement piece that quite literally reflects your love and your aesthetic. For this project, I've included one of my all-time favourite quotes: 'Together is a beautiful place to be.' It's sweet, timeless and perfectly captures what weddings are all about – being surrounded by all of your favourite people during one of life's most unforgettable moments.

Materials & Tools

- Mirror sign SVG file (see page 46)
- Cricut fine-point blade and housing
- 12 × 24in (30.5 × 61cm) LightGrip or StandardGrip cutting mat
- Cricut Value Vinyl (or adhesive vinyl of your choice)
- Extra-large mirror
- Greaseproof baking (parchment) paper
- Transfer tape roll
- Transparent tape (optional)
- Ruler or measuring tape
- Brayer
- Scissors
- Weeder
- Scraper

Compatible Machines

- Cricut Maker family
- Cricut Explore family

Base Material Settings

- Value Vinyl (or if you are using another vinyl, the appropriate setting for it)

Together is a beautiful place to be.
MARINA & ALASTAIR

1 Clean your mirror to ensure all fingerprints and any residue are removed. Next, download the SVG file (see page 46) and upload it into Design Space, then add this SVG to your Canvas screen.

2 Using a ruler or measuring tape, measure the area on your mirror where you wish to place your design. In Design Space, resize your design accordingly. If you want to cut from one piece of vinyl, the maximum size you can use for your design is 11.5 × 11.5in (29.2 × 29.2cm) or 11.5 × 23.5in (29.2 × 59.6cm), depending on your cutting mat size and whether you're using Value Vinyl or Smart Vinyl. If you don't mind cutting your design in two parts, then either part can be as large as these measurements.

3 You can use the design as it is or personalize it. To add a text box with names and/or date, select Text, then choose a font that you like from Design Space or your device; I used Design Space's Beloved font, which is available through Cricut Access or as a one-off purchase, but choose a font that suits your wedding style. I suggest a non-cursive font to create visual balance. Add your text, then move the text box to where you'd like it to be and make any adjustments to the text size, letter spacing, etc. If you have positioned the text underneath the design as I have, highlight both layers and select Align – Center Horizontally. If you're cutting your design in a single cut, select both layers and choose Attach. If cutting your design in two parts, don't choose Attach – use the aligned design as a visual reference to apply it to your mirror.

4 In Design Space, click Make to take you to the Prepare screen. Trim your vinyl to size and place it translucent plastic side down on your cutting mat; use a brayer to ensure they're adhered together if necessary. It can be difficult to see which is the translucent side if you are using white or a light-coloured Value Vinyl; peel back a small corner – the vinyl side is the brighter or bolder layer. Ensure the position of the design on your screen matches where the vinyl is on the cutting mat – you can click and drag the image on-screen if it isn't. When you're happy with everything, press Continue, then follow the on-screen instructions for your sign to be cut.

5 After your machine has finished, carefully separate the vinyl from the cutting mat. If you have chosen to do two cuts, repeat steps 4 to 5 for the second cut. Use your weeder tool to remove all the bits of vinyl that you do not want on your mirror – all that should be left on your carrier sheet is your final design.

6 Now apply the transfer tape. If your design is in two parts, align the two pieces to match your design on the Canvas screen, then tape them together on the back with transparent tape. Trim the transfer tape with scissors so it's slightly larger than your design, then fold down the top section of the backing sheet so that only a thin strip of transfer tape is visible. Place it lightly on top of your vinyl, then check and adjust the position of the tape if necessary. Once it is correctly aligned, slowly pull away the backing sheet, allowing the transfer tape to smoothly settle on top of the vinyl. Use the scraper tool to rub the transfer tape so your vinyl sticks to it. If it's not secure, flip the carrier sheet over and rub the other side. Now carefully peel the transfer tape and vinyl off of the vinyl's carrier sheet.

7 Because this is a large design, it can be difficult to place it perfectly on the first try – and once vinyl sticks, it's staying there! Use this greaseproof paper hack: cut a sheet of greaseproof paper slightly larger than your design and lay it on your work surface. Place the sticky side of your vinyl on the greaseproof paper, with the transfer sheet on top. Rub the transfer sheet with your hands or scraper tool over the layers for a light adhesion. This will give you some placement flexibility in the next steps.

8 To transfer the vinyl to your mirror, first fold down the top edge of the greaseproof paper so just a small strip of the sticky transfer tape is visible, then position it on your mirror without applying pressure. Adjust the position of your design so it's exactly where you want it, then slowly peel some of the greaseproof paper down without exposing the vinyl. Check and adjust the position of the transfer paper if necessary.

9 Once you're happy with the placement, slowly pull away the rest of the greaseproof paper, allowing the transfer tape and vinyl to settle onto the mirror. Now use your scraper tool to rub the transfer tape so the vinyl adheres to the mirror. Slowly peel back the transfer tape. If you see any air bubbles in your vinyl, place the greaseproof paper back on top and use your scraper tool again to work out any bubbles until you're happy. Don't underestimate using your fingernails as well for any tiny, fiddly areas! On the big day, place your mirror on an easel and decorate with florals to match your wedding style or ceremony decor.

PRO TIPS:

Because mirrors come in different sizes, you may wish to make a larger sign. If you need a vinyl size larger than the 12 × 12in (30.5 × 30.5cm) Value Vinyl sheets I've used, use Value Vinyl in roll format (if available in your country) or the almost unlimited length of Smart Vinyl. You can also cut this design word by word by using the Contour feature on the SVG layer. Contour hides specific cut lines; this allows you to control what your machine cuts from a single image or layer, so you can make entire words disappear and later reappear as you need them. It's a wonderful Design Space trick!

After the big day, just peel off the wording and upcycle the mirror as home decor!

You can use this same SVG for any pre-wedding event, such as signage, favours and T-shirts – it's a lovely quote to share in any medium.

Bouquet Ribbon

Inspired by Jane Austen's *Sense and Sensibility*, I've designed this bouquet ribbon project with one of its most famous quotes: 'My heart is and always will be yours.' My own inner Elinor Dashwood will never not get emotional with those words (spoken in Mr Hugh Grant's voice, of course), and they make for a beautiful wedding day sentiment as you walk down the aisle towards your beloved.

Materials & Tools

- Bouquet ribbon SVG file (see page 46)
- Cricut fine-point blade and housing
- Machine-specific Cricut LightGrip or StandardGrip cutting mat: 12 × 12in (30.5 × 30.5cm) for Maker or Explore; 4.5 × 12in (11.4 × 30.5cm) for Joy
- Cricut EasyPress Mini
- Cricut EasyPress heat-resistant mat
- Heat transfer vinyl (HTV)
- 60in (1.5m) strip of 2in (50mm) wide ribbon
- Measuring tape
- Brayer
- Weeder
- Trimmer and/or scissors
- Cardboard toilet paper tube or a ribbon spool (optional)

Compatible Machines

- Cricut Maker family
- Cricut Explore family
- Cricut Joy Xtra
- Cricut Joy

Base Material Settings

- Everyday Iron-On

heart
and always will be - yours

1 First, organize all your materials. Next, download the SVG file (see page 46) and upload it into Design Space, then add this SVG to your Canvas screen. The quote in the SVG is split over two layers in case you need to use two cutting mats or you decide to have it over two lines and not one.

2 Using a measuring tape, measure the area on your ribbon where you will want to place your design. For a balanced design, keep the quote in the middle, with an equal space between it and the top and bottom edges of the ribbon. In Design Space, resize your quote accordingly. My ribbon is 2in (50mm) wide, so I've resized the quote to be a height of 1.2in (3cm) in one continuous line, which made the length of the quote nearly 16in (41cm) long. Because I'm using 12 × 12in (30.5 × 30.5cm) mats, I've kept the two layers separate rather than use the Attach setting. If you're using a 12 × 24in (30.5 × 61cm) mat, you should highlight the two layers and select Attach.

3 In Design Space, click Make, then on the Prepare screen, turn on Mirror so the quote will read correctly on your ribbon after pressing. Trim a piece of HTV so that it is slightly larger than the quote and place it shiny side down on your cutting mat; use a brayer to ensure they're adhered together if necessary. If you're using two mats, trim two pieces of HTV to match the two halves of the quotes and place one on each mat. On the Prepare screen, make sure the position of the design on your screen matches the position of the HTV on the mat(s) – click and drag the design on-screen if they don't.

4 When you're happy with everything, press Continue, then follow the on-screen instructions for your text to be cut.

5 After your machine has finished, carefully separate the HTV from the cutting mat. Use your weeder tool to remove all the bits of HTV that you do not want on your ribbon – all that should be left are the letters.

6 Preheat your EasyPress Mini – you can use the Cricut Heat Guide (see page 16) to choose the correct setting for your fabric and HTV type, though I always use the lowest setting in 5-second intervals with delicate fabrics. Place your ribbon on your EasyPress mat, then position your HTV piece(s) shiny side up on your ribbon. It should be centred vertically, but it can be anywhere along the length (just not too close to the end, in case you find you need to trim the ribbon or it frays).

7 When your heat press is ready, press according to the recommended setting. Everything will be hot, so carefully remove the ribbon from the mat to allow it to cool completely. Once the carrier sheet is cool to the touch, slowly peel back to reveal the quote. For storage, wrap your ribbon around a toilet paper cardboard tube or ribbon spool to avoid creases before the wedding day.

PRO TIPS:

Not planning to carry a bouquet? These personalized ribbons are beautifully versatile – tie them around an 'In Loving Memory' floral arrangement, drape them on 'reserved' chair backs, or even weave them into a hand-fasting ceremony, which is what I did at my own wedding.

Go with what you love most when it comes to choosing the ribbon – satin, silk or chiffon all work beautifully with HTV. If you're unsure about the fabric type, always test it first. Ribbon length is all about personal style: some adore the long, romantic, flowy aesthetic, while others prefer a more modern, minimal look. With so many colour options available, it's easy to find ribbons to perfectly match your wedding palette. Consider choosing a wider ribbon for your personalization and adding thinner coordinating ribbons to wrap around your bouquet for an extra decorative touch.

If you use wider ribbons, you can stack the quote over two lines, but remember to highlight the two layers and select Attach on the Canvas screen before you press Make.

1
cricut

2

3
cricut

4
cricut explore 4

5

6

7
cricut

7

7

In Loving Memory Heart Patch

Weddings can be a bittersweet time when someone we love is no longer with us. Their physical absence is especially felt on a day meant for gathering, celebration and togetherness. To honour those who can't be present – in my case, my grandparents Nuna and Poppi, as seen and remembered in this project – this heart patch project offers a deeply personal way to keep their memory close as you walk down the aisle. Grief may never fully leave us, but creating something in tribute can be healing, memorable and a beautiful way to say, 'You are forever in my heart'.

Materials & Tools

- Heart patch SVG file (see page 46)
- Inkjet printer
- Cricut fine-point blade and housing
- Machine-specific Cricut LightGrip or StandardGrip cutting mat: 12 × 12in (30.5 × 30.5cm) for Maker or Explore
- Cricut EasyPress Mini or household iron
- Cricut EasyPress heat-resistant mat
- Cricut Printable Iron-On for Dark Fabrics
- Paper pressing sheet (included with the Printable Iron-On)
- Fabric heart sew-on patch
- Digital photo of your loved one(s)
- Ruler
- Brayer
- Lint roller
- Metal pin or brooch backing
- Hot glue gun and hot glue stick

Compatible Machines

- Cricut Maker family
- Cricut Explore family
- Cricut Joy Xtra

Base Material Settings

- Printable Iron-On, Dark

1 First, organize all your materials. If your heart-shaped patch is the same proportions as the SVG, download the SVG file (see page 46) and upload it into Design Space, then add this SVG to your Canvas screen. If the SVG isn't the right shape for your patch, take a photo of your patch with your smartphone and upload it into Design Space, using the Background Remover to leave just the shape of your patch and choosing Flat Graphic when prompted. You'll find this operation much quicker and less fiddly if you photograph your patch on a plain background in a contrasting colour. You can use this patch photo as a shape guide on your Canvas in later steps.

2 Calibrate your Cricut machine with your printer if you haven't done so already, or if you've been prompted to do so by Design Space. This ensures the cutting and printing processes will be in alignment.

3 On your Canvas screen, click Upload and follow the on-screen instructions for uploading your loved ones' photo, ensuring you select Flat Graphic towards the end so it will be a Print Then Cut image. There's no need to remove any of the background from the photo.

4 Using a ruler, measure the area of the patch where you plan to place your iron-on photo. In Design Space, resize your image accordingly. My patch is 4in (10cm) wide, so I resized my uploaded photo to about 5.25in (13.3cm) so that my grandparents' faces would fit nicely within the heart shape in the next step.

5 Next, resize your heart image to fit within your photo. Now place the heart shape on your photo where you want it to be – to do this, with only the heart layer selected, change the Operation to Guide, which will give you just the outline of your heart so you can see exactly what the cut photo will look like. You may need to rotate one of the images to get everything you want within the heart shape. To crop the photo to a heart shape, highlight both layers and click Slice. This creates a new Slice Result layer of your heart-shaped photo; keep this layer and delete the other two. Resize the photo to fit how you would like on your patch; my photo is 2.76 x 2.57in (7 x 6.5cm) as I wanted a lot of the floral pattern to show.

6 In Design Space, click Make to take you to the Prepare screen. If you're making more than one patch, change the Project Copies to the appropriate number and click Apply. When you're happy with everything, press Continue, then follow the on-screen instructions. You will be instructed to first insert the printable iron-on sheet into your printer; check your printer's manual to ensure you put the sheet in the correct paper feed tray.

7 After the heart-shaped photos have been printed, place the printable iron-on sheet on your cutting mat; use a brayer to ensure they're adhered together if necessary. Make sure its position matches your screen, then follow the rest of the on-screen instructions.

8 When your machine has finished, carefully separate the heart shapes from the sheet.

9 Preheat your EasyPress Mini – use the Cricut Heat Guide (see page 16) to choose the correct setting for your fabric and Printable Iron-On. While your machine preheats, use a lint roller to remove any lint or hair from your patch. Once your heat press has heated up, place your patch on your EasyPress mat and give it a 5-second preheat with the EasyPress Mini.

10 Place your design photo side up on your patch and cover it with your protective pressing sheet. Press according to the recommended settings. Remove your patch from the EasyPress mat and allow it to cool completely.

11 When the patch has cooled, use a hot glue gun to attach a metal pin or brooch backing to the back of your patch. On the big day, pin your patch onto your suit jacket's inner pocket, the inner liner of your wedding dress or wherever is most memorable for you. And after the big day, store it in your wedding keepsake box or pin it to another item of clothing.

PRO TIPS:

If you're buying a pre-made patch, look for 'sew-on' instead of 'iron-on', since heat pressing a Printable Iron-On photo onto an iron-on patch can get messy or cause issues with adhesion.

Instead of a pin, you can hand-sew your patch onto your attire if you want to make it permanent. You can also add some lovely, colourful personalized embroidery details for an even more special touch.

1
HI-TACK

4

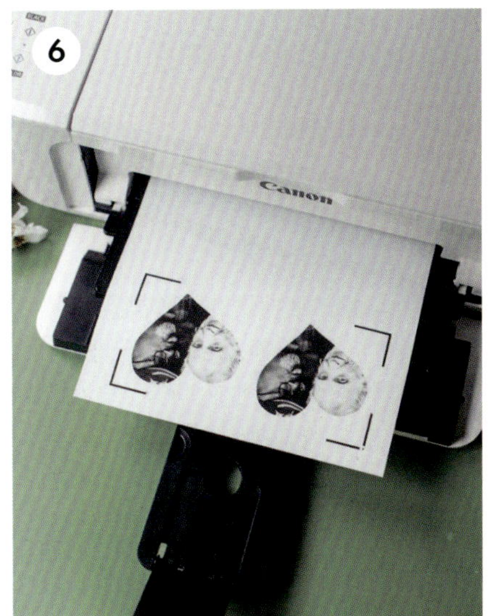
6
Canon

7
cricut joy xtra

8

9

9

10

11
HI-TACK

Fabric Bar Menu Sign

Make a stylish statement at your wedding bar with a hanging fabric drink menu sign. Not only does this large-scale piece free up valuable counter space, but it also adds a soft, elegant touch to your decor. And because every project has a little story behind it, I couldn't resist including my and Mr B's own wedding signature cocktail in this project: Pickles' Punch – named after my number one feline sidekick, who also hopped the pond with me.

Materials & Tools

- Bar menu SVG file (see page 46)
- Cricut fine-point blade and housing
- Cricut roll holder (optional)
- Machine-specific Cricut StandardGrip cutting mat (if not using a full-width roll of Smart Iron-On): 12 × 12in (30.5 × 30.5cm) for Maker or Explore; 4.5 × 12in (11.4 × 30.5cm) for Joy
- Cricut EasyPress or Cricut Autopress
- Cricut EasyPress heat-resistant mat
- Cricut Smart Iron-On, in Gold, or regular heat transfer vinyl (HTV)
- Large piece of fabric – at least dishcloth-sized
- Heat-resistant tape
- Measuring tape
- Brayer (if using a cutting mat)
- Weeder
- Lint roller

Compatible Machines

- Cricut Maker family
- Cricut Explore family
- Cricut Joy Xtra
- Cricut Joy

Base Material Settings

- Smart Iron-On Matless Heat Transfer Vinyl (or if you are using a different HTV, the appropriate setting for it)

Cheers to Love
Signature Cocktail
Pickles' Punch
Wine
Pinot Grigio
Chardonnay
Merlot
Beer
IPA
Lager
Stout
Spirits
Gin
Tequila
Vodka
Bourbon
Soft Drinks
Cola
Ginger Ale
Lemon Lime
Sparkling Water

1 First, organize all your materials. Next, download the SVG file (see page 46) and upload it into Design Space, then add this SVG to your Canvas screen. The SVG file includes multiple drink categories – select Ungroup, then delete or hide any layers that you don't need.

2 Using a measuring tape, measure the area on your sign for placing your design. Ensure there's enough blank space above it so your sign can be held in place by a floral arrangement or bottles without any words being covered. As it's a bar sign that should be seen, I've sized my design to be 11.7in (29.7cm) wide to fit my fabric. To help guide the spacing and sizing your text, add a rectangle shape to your Canvas, and resize it to the exact size of your fabric. You'll delete this shape before cutting (you'll get a red warning icon on the layer as it's too big to be cut).

3 To add a text box, select Text, then choose a font that you like from Design Space or your device; I used Design Space's Beloved font, which is available through Cricut Access or as a one-off purchase, but choose a font that suits your wedding. I recommend using a non-cursive font to create visual balance with the SVG's script lettering and makes your menu easier to read from a distance. Type out the names of each drink being served and place the text box under the appropriate category – align and centre the boxes as needed and make any adjustments to the text size, letter spacing, etc. Repeat this step for the drinks under each of the other drink categories. If you're using Maker or Explore, highlight all the layers and click Attach once you're happy with how it looks. (You don't need to attach the layers if using Joy or Joy Xtra.)

4 In Design Space, click Make to take you to the Prepare screen. On the Prepare screen, select Mirror as your design should be cut in reverse. If you're not using Smart Materials or your Smart Iron-On roll isn't its original size, place the material shiny side down on your cutting mat and use a brayer to ensure they're adhered together if necessary. Ensure the position of the design on your screen matches the position of the material on the mat – click and drag the images on-screen if they don't.

5 When you're happy with everything, press Continue, then follow the on-screen instructions. It will now prompt you to feed your Smart Iron-On shiny side down directly into your cutting machine or otherwise cut the reduced-sized Smart Iron-On or other HTV being used.

6 After your machine has finished, carefully separate the Smart Iron-On or HTV from the cutting mats if you're using them. Use your weeder tool to remove all of the bits from the carrier sheets that you do not want on your sign – all that should be left on the carrier sheets are the words.

7 Preheat your EasyPress – use Cricut Heat Guide (see page 16) to choose the correct setting for your fabric and Smart Iron-On or HTV. Meanwhile, use a lint roller to remove any lint from the fabric. Place your fabric on your heat-resistant mat. Once the heat press has heated up, remove any wrinkles in your fabric with EasyPress, then place your design shiny side up on your fabric. If using Joy or Joy Xtra, or you cut your sections individually, place each piece on the fabric and arrange them how you would like them to look. Because you will be pressing your design in multiple sections, use heat-resistant tape along the carrier sheet's edges on all the pieces to prevent the design from shifting.

8 Place your EasyPress on top of the first section of your design and press the GO button. Using firm pressure, move it across the first section until it beeps. Repeat for each section until all of the fabric has been pressed. Remove from the mat, allow to cool, then slowly peel back the carrier sheet(s). You may need to reheat any areas of Smart Iron-On or HTV that didn't adhere fully. If so, place the carrier sheet back over it, and re-press in 5-second intervals. Once everything is cool to the touch, slowly peel back the carrier sheet. To store your lovely bar menu fabric sign, roll it around a gift wrap cardboard tube and use spare ribbon or hair ties to secure.

PRO TIPS:

Want to skip the heat press thing? Make this project with adhesive vinyl and a non-fabric surface such as an acrylic sheet or a mirror.

When pressing designs larger than your EasyPress, look for linear breaks in the design to determine the sections to individually heat press.

If using a pre-loved fabric remnant where edges aren't quite straight or tidy to begin with, trim the edges using an acrylic ruler and fabric scissors or a rotary cutter and a self-healing mat.

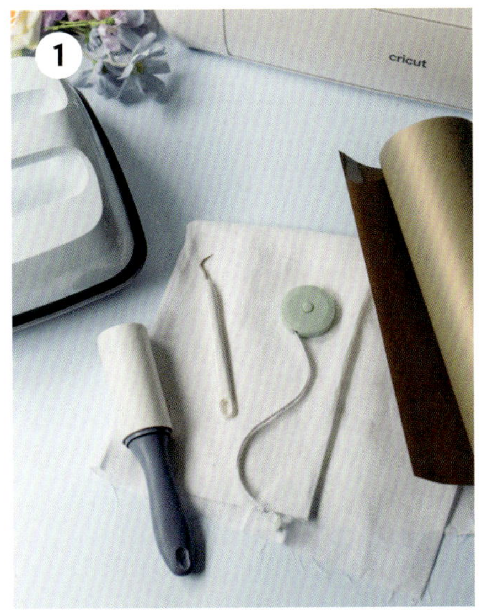
1
cricut

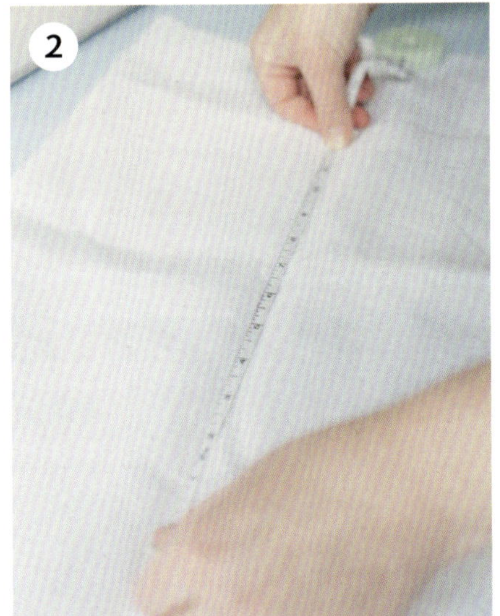
2

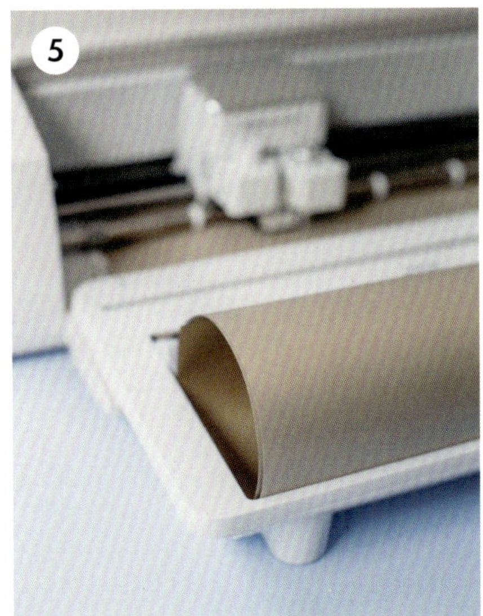
5

5
cricut

6
PUNCH

7
cricut

7

8
GIN
TEQUILA
VODKA
BOURBON

8

Signature Cocktail Straw Flags

Even the drinks get their own DIY! Dress up your signature cocktail or beverage of choice with a stylish straw flag. Cricut Smart Paper Sticker Cardstock is one of my top favourite materials to craft with for its versatility – no glue is needed as it already has its own adhesive backing. One of the best parts about this simple project is that it can be done when you don't have a lot of time but still want to include a thoughtful detail for your cocktail hour. A good rule of thumb for wedding planning is to make at least one special straw per guest (as your bartender will likely have other straws). Any leftovers can be used for future home parties, so nothing goes to waste. Sip sip hooray!

Materials & Tools

- Cocktail straw flags SVG file (see page 46)
- Cricut fine-point blade and housing
- 0.3mm black extra fine point pen
- Machine-specific LightGrip cutting mat (if not using full-width Smart materials): 12 × 12in (30.5 × 30.5cm) for Maker or Explore; 4.5 × 12in (11.4 × 30.5cm) for Joy
- Cricut Smart Paper Sticker Cardstock, in White (or plain cardstock of your choice)
- Brayer
- Glue tape runner (if not using Smart Paper Sticker Cardstock)
- Paper straws

Compatible Machines

- Cricut Maker family
- Cricut Explore family
- Cricut Joy Xtra (see Pro Tips overleaf)
- Cricut Joy

Base Material Settings

- Smart Paper Matless Sticker Cardstock (or if you are using a different cardstock, the appropriate setting for it)

Size & Quantity

If you intend to use the SVG file at its original size, which is correct for standard-sized straws, you should be able to fit 12 flags on a 12 × 12in (30.5 × 30.5cm) sheet of Smart Paper Sticker Cardstock or regular cardstock.

SIP SIP
HOORAY
sip sip hooray

1 First, organize all your materials. Next, download the SVG file (see page 46) and upload it into Design Space, then add this SVG to your Canvas screen. The design is the correct size for standard straws, so it doesn't need to be adjusted unless you prefer to make flags of a different size.

2 For all the layers with text, click on the Operation drop-down menu and select Pen (you need to tell your machine to write rather than cut these layers). Next, highlight all the layers and select Attach.

3 In Design Space, click Make to take you to the Prepare screen. Change the number of Project Copies to however many will fit on a single sheet of the cardstock you're using and click Apply. For your Smart Paper Sticker Cardstock, adjust and move the flags on your screen as needed to fit on your sheet. If you are not using Smart materials or your Smart Paper Sticker Cardstock sheet isn't its original width, place your material on the cutting mat and use a brayer to ensure they're adhered together if necessary. Make sure the positions of the designs on your screen match the positions of your materials on the mats – click and drag the images on-screen if they don't.

4 When you're happy with everything, press Continue, then follow the on-screen instructions for your flags to be written and cut. You will now be prompted to feed your Smart Paper Sticker Cardstock grid side down directly into your cutting machine or on your cutting mat.

5 If you're using a cutting mat, carefully separate it from the cardstock when the machine has finished. Repeat steps 3 to 5 as many times as needed to make the number of flags you want for your cocktail hour.

6 To make the Smart Paper Sticker Cardstock flags, peel off each flag from the carrier sheet, partially fold it in half by placing both ends together, and then slide a straw into and against the loop end. Ensure it's not too close to the top of the straw to allow for unobstructed sipping. If you're using a different cardstock that doesn't have an adhesive backing, run a strip of glue tape on the inside of one half of the flag; with this method, you may also need additional adhesive on the straw itself, depending on your straw type and how tight the flag is on your straw. Securely press down the sticker cardstock so it stays on your straw. Cheers to one of the easiest DIYs you'll do for your wedding!

PRO TIPS:

The SVG is very customizable – you could delete the text layers and replace them with text boxes for your wedding date, the signature cocktail name or any other sentiment you love.

Smart Paper Sticker Cardstock and extra fine point pens come in myriad other colours as well, so these chic straw flags can be very personalized to your unique vision.

There is currently no Joy Xtra-sized Smart Paper Sticker Cardstock, so if you are using Joy Xtra and you'd like to use that material, you will need to utilize a cutting mat and trim to size as needed.

1
cricut

4
cricut maker 3

4
SIP SIP
HOORAY

6
SIP SIP
HOORAY
sip sip hooray
Sip Sip Hooray

6
sip sip hooray

6
sip sip hooray

6
sip sip hooray

Photo Frame Table Numbers

During our own pandemic-era wedding, Mr B and I had to plan two different events – one in the USA for my American loved ones and another in the UK for his British family. When we held our Virginia picnic reception later that year, we displayed printed photos from our English wedding to help tie our two worlds together. That experience inspired this table number project: a way to blend two meaningful moments into one special detail for the big day. Whether your photos are from an elopement, engagement, holiday or another meaningful milestone, these acrylic block frame table numbers offer both a sentimental touch and a practical purpose – helping your guests find their seats while showcasing your favourite memories.

Materials & Tools

- Table numbers SVG file (see page 46)
- Cricut fine-point blade and housing
- Machine-specific Cricut LightGrip or StandardGrip cutting mat: 12 × 12in (30.5 × 30.5cm) for Maker or Explore; 4.5 × 12in (11.4 × 30.5cm) for Joy
- Cricut Value Vinyl (or vinyl of your choice), in a colour that contrasts with your photo
- Transfer tape
- 4 × 6in (10 × 15cm) acrylic block magnetic photo frames
- 4 × 6in (10 × 15cm) printed photos of you and your beloved
- Ruler
- Brayer
- Scissors
- Weeder
- Scraper

Compatible Machines

- Cricut Maker family
- Cricut Explore family
- Cricut Joy Xtra
- Cricut Joy

Base Material Settings

- Value Vinyl (or if using another vinyl, the appropriate setting for it)

5

1 First, organize all your materials. Next, download the SVG file (see page 46) and upload it into Design Space, then add this SVG to your Canvas screen. The SVG file has the numbers one to twelve both spelt out and in numerals, each on a separate layer – delete any that you don't need. There is also a zero numeral, in case you need to create additional table numbers.

2 To help you decide how big to make the numbers and where they will look best on your frames, place the photos in the frames. Using a ruler, measure the area on your frame where you want to place your number. In Design Space, resize your numbers accordingly. I've made my numerals 3in (7.6cm) tall.

3 In Design Space, click Make to take you to the Prepare screen. Adjust the position of each number to ensure you use the minimum amount of material – but also ensure there will be enough space to cut them out with scissors later. Trim the sheet of vinyl so that it is slightly larger than all the numbers and place it translucent plastic side down on your cutting mat; use a brayer to ensure they're adhered together if necessary. It can be difficult to see which is the translucent side if you are using white or a light-coloured Value Vinyl; peel back a small corner – the vinyl side is the brighter or bolder layer. On the Prepare screen, make sure the position of the numbers on your screen matches the position of the vinyl on the mat – click and drag the images on-screen if they don't.

4 When you're happy with everything, press Continue, then follow the on-screen instructions for your numbers to be cut.

5 After your machine has finished, carefully separate the vinyl from the cutting mat. Use your weeder tool to remove all of the bits of vinyl that you do not want (for easier removal, cut off large sections with scissors) – all that should be left on your carrier sheet are your numbers. Cut out each number (still on the carrier sheet) using scissors.

6 Trim a piece of transfer tape the same size as one of the numbers on its carrier sheet and remove its backing sheet. You can reuse this same piece of transfer tape for every table number, so save the backing sheet. Place it on the vinyl and use your scraper tool to ensure they're stuck together, then peel away the carrier sheet.

7 Carefully place your transfer tape with one of the numbers on a photo frame. Once you are happy with its position, rub the transfer tape with your scraper tool so your number fully adheres to your frame, then slowly peel back the transfer tape. Repeat steps 6 to 7 for all the remaining numbers.

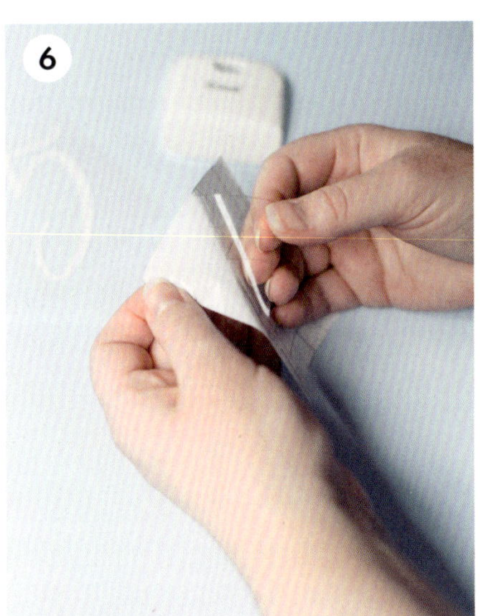

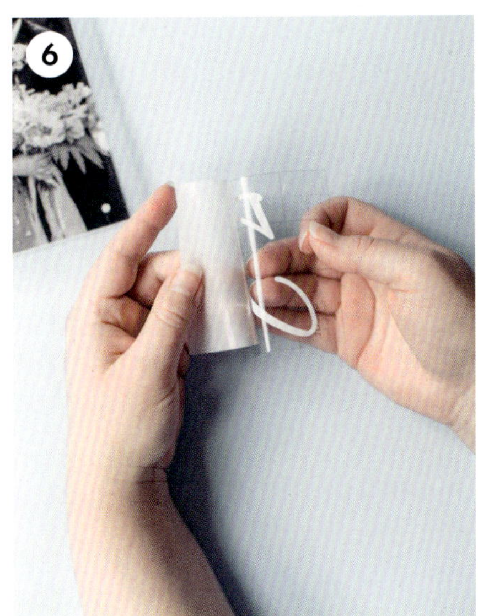

PRO TIP:

When it comes to choosing a vinyl colour that is easily seen by guests, a classic white vinyl always looks great on both colour and black-and-white prints, and a nice bright metallic is another timeless neutral. Save your leftover vinyl pieces in case extra tables are added later and you need more table numbers.

Favour Boxes

No guest goes home empty-handed with this sweet, peony-inspired favour box! If you're including favours on your big day, why not make them extra special with a handmade touch? This project is a beautiful way to show your love and gratitude to the people who are celebrating with you – wrapped up in a little box of joy. These favour boxes are the perfect size for sweet treats such as candy, chocolates, mini cookies or even something more unique like DIY spice blends or pet goodies for guests to take home to their furry friends. The best favours are the ones that feel personal, so have fun with it and let both of your personalities shine through. Make it crafty, make it meaningful, make it you.

Materials & Tools

- Favour box SVG file (see page 46)
- Cricut fine-point blade and housing
- Cricut scoring stylus
- Machine-specific Cricut LightGrip cutting mat: 12 × 12in (30.5 × 30.5cm) for Maker or Explore
- 80lb (216gsm) textured coloured cardstock
- 16in (41cm) strip of 1in (25mm) wide ribbon
- Brayer
- Scissors
- Scraper
- Quick-drying craft glue
- Scoring board and bone folder, or Cricut Portable Trimmer with a scoring blade (if using a Joy Xtra)

Compatible Machines

- Cricut Maker family
- Cricut Explore family
- Cricut Joy Xtra

Base Material Settings

- Medium Cardstock (80lb/216gsm)

Size & Quantity

If you intend to use the SVG file at its original size, one 12 × 12in (30.5 × 30.5cm) sheet of textured cardstock will make one favour box.

1 First, organize all your materials. Next, download the SVG file (see page 46) and upload it into Design Space, then add this SVG to your Canvas screen.

2 On the layer that looks like a sideways ladder, update the operation to Score. This layer should then appear with dotted lines. Next, highlight both layers and click Attach. If you are using Joy Xtra, which doesn't support the Score operation, you will need to delete the SVG's score lines layer and manually create your own fold lines after cutting. I recommend using a papercraft scoring board and bone folder or the Cricut Portable Trimmer with the scoring blade for this – you will be making a lot of these boxes!

3 Place your chosen cardstock on your cutting mat; use a brayer to ensure they're adhered together if necessary. In Design Space, click Make to take you to the Prepare screen. If everything looks correct, press Continue, then follow the on-screen instructions for your boxes to be scored and cut.

4 After your machine has finished, carefully separate the cardstock from the cutting mat. Gently scrape off the leftover bits of card with your scraper tool or fingernails. Repeat steps 3 to 4 as many times as needed to match your guest list.

5 To assemble the boxes, use your scraper tool to crease the pre-scored lines to create a good fold. Apply a thin line of craft glue to the tab on the side, then attach the tab to the opposite side of the box and hold it until the glue has dried. Repeat for all the other boxes.

6 Fold the bottom flaps into themselves to form each of your boxes, then fill them with your favourite treat. Tie a piece of ribbon to the top flaps to secure the box shut. Now you're ready to spoil your guests with a handmade goodie to take home!

PRO TIPS:

This makes a great group project. Gather your VIPs for a 'crafternoon' to assemble these boxes. Pre-cut everything before they arrive to make it a streamlined fun day for everyone.

Depending on your time and budget, you could also create little paper topper tags with a 'thank you' message, or you could even iron-on 'with love' on your box ribbons for a lovely extra touch.

4

5
Cricut

5

5

6

6

6

Floral Place Cards

Your guests will fall in love with the shimmering beauty of these gold-foiled reception place cards. Using real wood veneer and some cardstock, you can create a small wow factor detail at each guest's place setting, and it makes for a lovely keepsake for guests to take home with them. The peony motif helps to tie all of the stationery projects together for a cohesive wedding design.

Materials & Tools

- Place cards SVG file (see page 46)
- Cricut fine-point blade and housing (for the cardstock)
- Cricut deep-point blade and housing (for the wood veneer)
- 12 × 12in (30.5 × 30.5cm) LightGrip cutting mat
- 12 × 12in (30.5 × 30.5cm) StrongGrip cutting mat
- Cricut foil transfer kit (using the fine tip)
- Cricut foil tape (supplied with the transfer kit), or another tape with a light adhesive
- Cricut foil transfer sheets, in Gold
- Cricut natural wood veneer, in Maple
- 60lb (160gsm) smooth white cardstock
- Glue dots
- Brayer
- Spatula

Compatible Machines

- Cricut Maker family
- Cricut Explore family

Base Material Settings

- Light Cardstock (65lb/176gsm) for the cardstock
- Natural Wood Veneer for the wood veneer

Size & Quantity

If you intend to use the SVG file at its original size, a 12 × 12in (30.5 × 30.5cm) foil transfer sheet and a sheet of wood veneer the same size will make 66 peonies, while an A4 sheet of smooth cardstock will make 22 place cards and a US letter-size sheet of smooth cardstock will make 20 place cards.

Damaris

1 First, organize all your materials. Next, download the SVG file (see page 46) and upload it into Design Space, then add this SVG to your Canvas screen. These place cards are a standard wedding place card size of 3.5in (9cm) wide. If you resize the cards, consider where you'll be placing them; for example, if they will be on or next to plates, measure the plates before you finalize the cards' size.

2 For the layer with the flower line details, click on the Operation drop-down menu and select Foil > Fine, leaving the other layers as Basic Cut.

3 To add a name to the card, select Text, then choose a font that you like from Design Space or your device; I used Design Space's DTC Cottage Style font in its Writing style, which is available through Cricut Access or as a one-off purchase, but choose a Writing-compatible font that suits your wedding. Move the text box so it sits over your white card layer. Add your guest's name and adjust the font size if necessary. Next, with the layer selected, click on the Operation drop-down menu and select Foil > Fine. If you see an outline of your text (and not one single line as if drawn with a pen), you will need to change the font style to Writing under the Font Style drop-down menu. If that option isn't available, choose a different font that does have a Writing style. You may find the Fine Foil setting reverts to Pen, in which case reselect Foil > Fine.

4 Click and highlight the guest's name and blank place card layers, then select Attach. If all the layers become attached rather than just the two you selected, undo the Attach command, ungroup all your layers, then select just the text and place card layers and select Attach. Highlight all the layers and select Group, then select Duplicate to create a new guest's place card with the same settings as the first one. Grouping helps keep bulk making in large numbers organized. Now select the text layer, choose Edit Text (or double click on the text) and replace the text with the next guest's name. Keep repeating this step until you've added all the remaining guests' names. You may wish to work in batches – see page 146.

5 In Design Space, click Make to take you to the Prepare screen. Place your wood veneer on your StrongGrip cutting mat and smooth it with your brayer. Place a foil transfer sheet tightly on top of the veneer, shiny side up, then secure it with the kit's white foil tape strips, ensuring you avoid any areas where the foiling tip will press down. Place your cardstock on your LightGrip cutting mat and secure a foil transfer sheet to it in exactly the same way.

6 On your machine's mobile device slot, line up your foil transfer housing, fine-point blade and deep-point blade so they are to hand. When you're happy with everything, press Continue, then follow the on-screen instructions. Design Space will tell you not to unload your mat between the foiling and cutting operations – this is important for accurate cutting after the foiling has been done!

7 After your machine has finished, carefully separate the cardstock and the veneer from the cutting mats. Use the spatula tool to avoid damaging the wood veneer when you lift it off the StrongGrip mat.

8 Place a small glue dot sticker on the peony-shaped end of the cardstock and put the wood veneer floral on top. Repeat for all the place cards, then store for your big day!

PRO TIPS:

You may find your cutting mat has gold highlights after your project, as the foil sheet incidentally touches the sticky parts. I suggest having one mat dedicated to foil projects.

The white foil tape is reusable. When Design Space tells you to remove the foil, carefully remove the tape as well and stick it back on its backing sheet for next time. Trim off any areas that are no longer usable.

If using a font from your device, ensure that it is a monoline font for the best foil writing results.

At the time of writing, the Foil functionality is currently not available or supported via the Design Space mobile app. You will need to use the desktop version to make this project.

If using a non-Cricut wood veneer, do some online research before you start, as some veneers may require different cut settings. Cricut Natural Wood Veneer was specifically formulated for use with the deep-point blade and Cricut cutting machines.

1
5
5
6
6
6
6
7
8

Wedding Sneaker Bow Clips

If you're like me with wide, wonky feet, you'll know finding cute wedding shoes can be a challenge. What if you need to go the comfort footwear route, especially for the reception, but still want to make it wedding pretty? That's where shoe bow clips come in! Removable and personalizable, you can add your name, new initials, wedding date or even just some symbols to these accessories. You can either buy pre-made bow clips or you can make your own with some satin ribbon and metal shoe clips.

Materials & Tools

- Heart patch SVG file (see page 46) (optional)
- Cricut fine-point blade and housing
- Machine-specific Cricut LightGrip or StandardGrip cutting mat: 12 × 12in (30.5 × 30.5cm) for Maker or Explore; 4.5 × 12in (11.4 × 30.5cm) for Joy
- Cricut EasyPress Mini
- Cricut EasyPress heat-resistant mat
- Heat transfer vinyl (HTV)
- Satin bow shoe clips
- Measuring tape or ruler
- Brayer
- Weeder

Compatible Machines

- Cricut Maker family
- Cricut Explore family
- Cricut Joy Xtra
- Cricut Joy

Base Material Settings

- Everyday Iron-On

MRS B

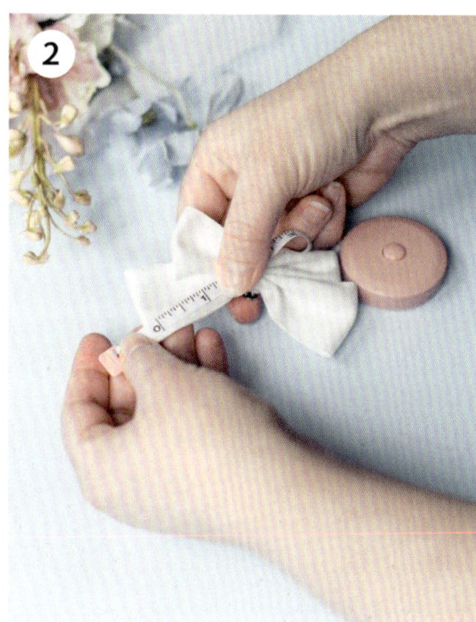

1 First, organize all your materials. Because you will want to personalize this project, it doesn't have its own dedicated SVG file. I have used the heart-shaped SVG file from the In Loving Memory Heart Patch project (see pages 108–111). If you are doing the same and you have already uploaded this file into Design Space, click Upload, select the image, and Add to Canvas; otherwise, download the SVG file (see page 46) and upload it into Design Space, then add this SVG to your Canvas screen, or choose your own design and load it into Design Space in the same way.

2 Using a measuring tape or ruler, measure the area on your bows where you will want to place your designs.

3 To add personalized text, select Text, then choose a font that you like from Design Space or your device; I used Design Space's BFC Dahlia Garden font, which is available through Cricut Access or as a one-off purchase, but choose a font that suits the style of your wedding. Because the text will be tiny – my text is just 0.25in (0.635cm) tall – I recommend using a chunky font that has a consistent line thickness so your Cricut cutting machine will cut without any issues. Once you have written your text, make any adjustments to the text size, letter spacing, etc. Highlight your layers and click Attach to keep your design together. Repeat this step to add a text box for the other bow.

4 In Design Space, click Make, then on the Prepare screen, turn on Mirror so the designs will read correctly on your bows after pressing. Trim a piece of HTV so that it is slightly larger than your design and place it shiny side down on your cutting mat; use a brayer to ensure they're adhered together if necessary. Make sure the position of the HTV on the mat matches the position of the design on your screen – you can click and drag the image on the screen if they don't. When you're happy with everything, press Continue, then follow the on-screen instructions for your designs to be cut.

5 After your machine has finished, carefully separate the HTV from the cutting mat. Use your weeder tool to remove all the bits of HTV that you do not want on your bows – all that should be left on your carrier sheet are the designs.

6 Preheat your EasyPress Mini – you can use the Cricut Heat Guide (see page 16) to choose the correct setting for your fabric and HTV type, though I always use the lowest setting in 5-second intervals with delicate fabrics. Place a bow on your EasyPress mat, then place your HTV design shiny side up on your bow.

7 Once your heat press has heated up, press according to the recommended settings. Remove the bow from the mat to allow it to cool completely. Repeat steps 6 to 7 for the second bow. Once the carrier sheets are cool to touch, slowly peel them back and then clip your bows onto your dancing shoes!

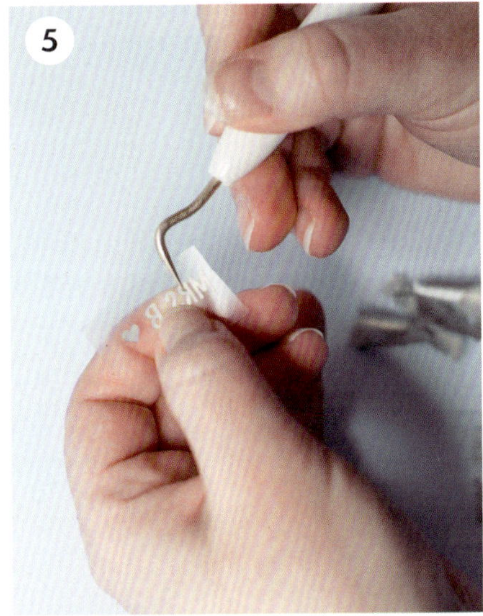

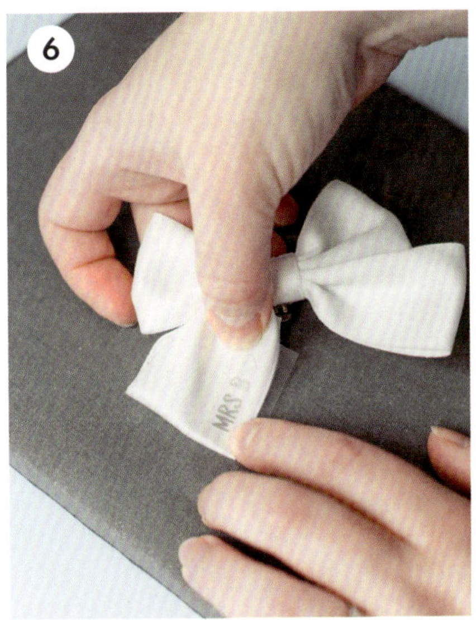

PRO TIPS:

You can use this personalized bow idea on almost anything – perhaps you would like to wear a ribbon bow in your hair or on a dress for your pre-wedding party, or have a special hidden detail on the inside of your wedding day attire.

While a memorable detail, it is also a tiny one – making it a great scrap project for using up leftover HTV from one of your other Cricut projects.

Just Married Hats

Embrace the cuteness of being 'just married' by making matching hats for your honeymoon! It's common knowledge that newlywed joy is contagious and may even get you some perks when travelling to your destination, so hey, why not lean into the fun while also getting some sun protection? And, of course, it makes for the sweetest photo memories of your honeymoon together. So, whether you're a baseball cap or bucket hat kind of couple, create this one in your own style.

Materials & Tools

- Just married hats SVG file (see page 46)
- Cricut fine-point blade and housing
- Machine-specific LightGrip or StandardGrip cutting mat (if using full-width sheets of Smart Iron-On): 12 × 12in (30.5 × 30.5cm) for Maker or Explore; 4.5 × 12 in (11.4 × 30.5cm) for Joy
- Cricut EasyPress Mini or Cricut Hat Press
- Hat pressing form or cotton hand towel
- Cricut Smart Iron-On, in White, or regular heat transfer vinyl (HTV)
- Plain baseball caps
- Strong heat-resistant tape
- Measuring tape
- Brayer
- Scissors or trimmer
- Weeder
- Lint roller

Compatible Machines

- Cricut Maker family
- Cricut Explore family
- Cricut Joy Xtra
- Cricut Joy

Base Material Settings

- Smart Iron-On Matless Heat Transfer Vinyl (or if using a different HTV, the appropriate setting for it)

just married

1 First, organize all your materials. Next, download the SVG file (see page 46) and upload it into Design Space, then add this SVG to your Canvas screen. The SVG file for this project has 'just' and 'married' in two different layers; arrange them depending on the size and shape of your hats and the look you wish to achieve. You will then need to select both layers and choose Attach so your machine will cut the words together as you've set them.

2 Using a measuring tape, measure the area on your hat where you wish to place your 'Just Married' design. In Design Space, resize your design accordingly. Once you're happy with the design, click Duplicate to add your second 'Just Married' design.

3 In Design Space, click Make, then on the Prepare screen, turn on Mirror so the designs will read correctly on your hats after pressing. If you are not using Smart Materials or your Smart Iron-On roll isn't its original width, trim two pieces of HTV or leftover pieces of Smart Iron-On so they are slightly larger than your designs, then place them shiny side down on your cutting mat; use a brayer to ensure they're adhered together if necessary. Ensure the positions of the material on the mat match the positions of the designs on your screen – you can click and drag the images on-screen if they don't.

4 When you're happy with everything, press Continue, then follow the on-screen instructions for your designs to be cut. It will now prompt you to feed your Smart Iron-On shiny side down directly into your cutting machine.

5 After your machine has finished, unload the Smart Iron-On, or if using a mat, unload the mat and carefully separate the HTV from it. Using scissors or a trimmer, cut out the design areas of the HTV (save the rest of the HTV for other projects). Use your weeder tool to remove all the bits of material that you do not want on your hats – all that should be left on your carrier sheet are the designs.

6 Preheat your EasyPress Mini – you can use the Cricut Heat Guide (see page 16) to choose the correct setting for your fabric and Smart Iron-On or type of HTV. While your machine preheats, use a lint roller to remove any lint from the hats. Place your first hat on your hat pressing form or a folded hand towel, making sure it's a snug fit. Place one of the designs shiny side up onto your hat and use some heat-resistant tape around the edges to keep it in place.

7 Once your heat press has heated up, move it over your Smart Iron-On or HTV in a side-to-side motion to heat the whole design. Allow it to cool completely. Once the carrier sheet is cool to the touch, carefully remove the heat-resistant tape and set it aside for the next hat, then slowly peel back the carrier sheet.

8 Depending on your hat's fabric and how it was manufactured, you may need to reheat any bits of Smart Iron-On or HTV that haven't adhered fully to your fabric. If so, place the carrier sheet back over your design, and re-press in 5-second intervals, allowing it to cool down fully before peeling back each time. Do this until all of your design stays cleanly on your fabric. Repeat steps 6 to 8 for your second hat. Once all finished, pack away your hats until you're ready to enjoy the sunshine together!

PRO TIP:

This project's SVG can go beyond a hat – if you want to be that adorable couple on your adventures, make matching T-shirts, beach bags and swimwear. You're only 'just married' for a short amount of time, so channel and own that beautiful, playful energy into whatever you make.

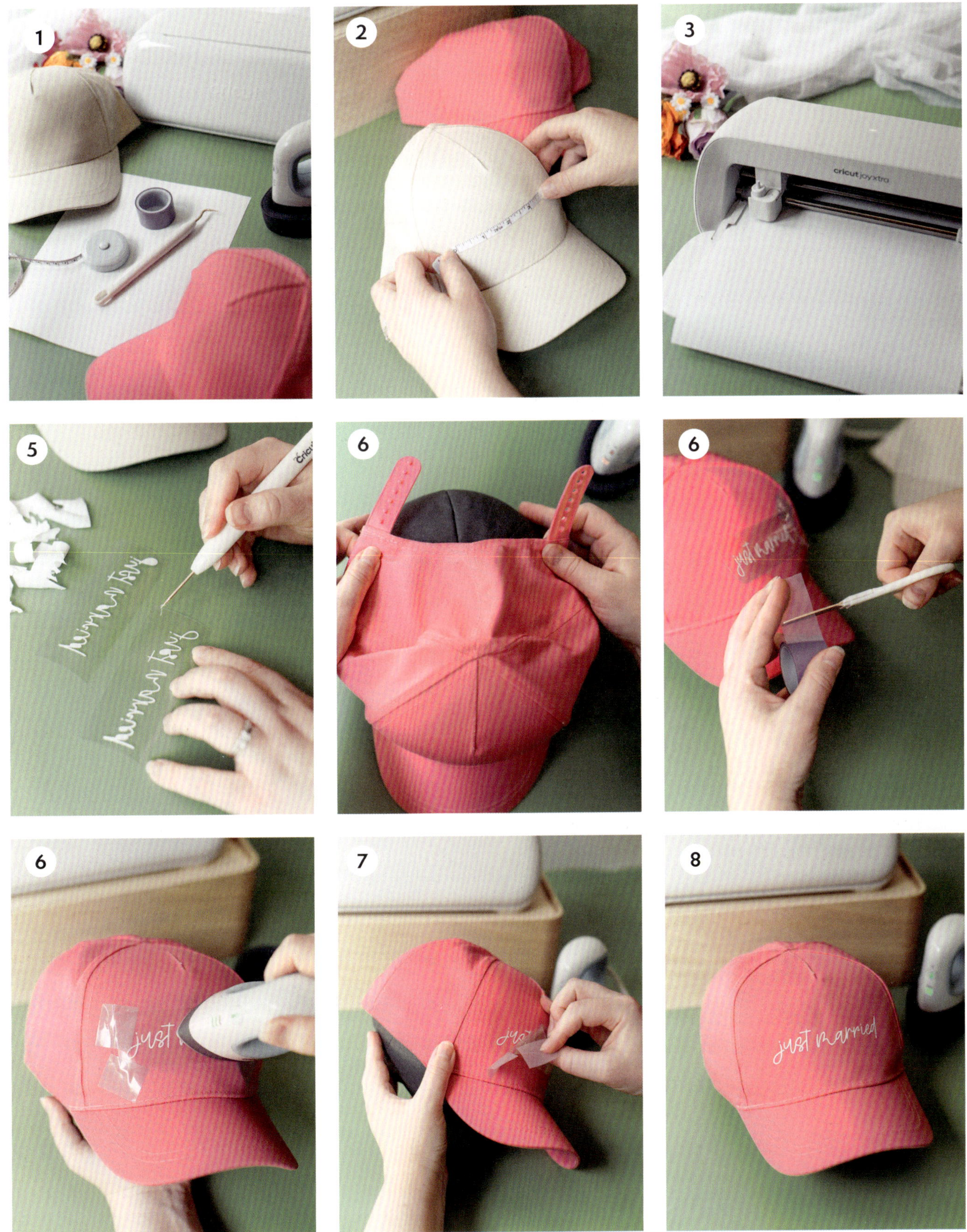
1
2
3
cricut joy xtra
5
6
6
6
just
7
8
just married

Honeymoon Luggage Tags

Jet off in personalized newlywed style! Decorate your suitcase, beach bag or backpack with this lovely leather luggage tag project. Whether you're a ribbon bow or bow tie kind of couple, mix and match your preferred details in your choice of HTV and leather with my ready-to-make SVG file. Happy honeymooning, lovebirds!

Materials & Tools

- Luggage tag SVG file (see page 46)
- Cricut fine-point blade and housing (for the HTV)
- Cricut deep-point blade and housing (for the leather)
- 12 × 12in (30.5 × 30.5cm) LightGrip or StandardGrip cutting mat
- 12 × 12in (30.5 × 30.5cm) StrongGrip cutting mat
- Cricut EasyPress Mini
- Cricut EasyPress heat-resistant mat
- Heat transfer vinyl (HTV)
- Cricut Genuine Leather (or tooling leather or vegan leather option; see Tips on page 142)
- Brayer
- Weeder
- Masking tape (optional)

Compatible Machines

- Cricut Maker family
- Cricut Explore family

Base Material Settings

- Metallic Leather for the leather
- Everyday Iron-On for the HTV

Mr &
Mrs

1 First, organize all your materials. Next, download the SVG file (see page 46) and upload it into Design Space, then add this SVG to your Canvas screen. The SVG file includes a variety of bow styles and abbreviated titles in addition to the luggage tag itself – delete or hide the layers you don't need. The SVG is already the correct size, but feel free to enlarge or reduce it in size if you wish.

2 Ungroup the layers, then resize and arrange the bow and the titles on your luggage tag as you wish. If they disappear behind the tag, simply select the tag and choose 'Send to Back'. Once satisfied, click and highlight the bow and titles layers, but not the luggage tag, and select Attach. If you are making multiple tags, select Duplicate for any applicable layers and repeat this step for the other tag(s).

3 When cutting thick materials like leather, you will need to move your Cricut machine's star wheels (the white rings on the metal roller) to the right side of the roller, so they are clear of the leather.

4 In Design Space, click Make, then on the Prepare screen, turn on Mirror so both your leather and HTV cuts are in reverse. Trim the leather and HTV so they're slightly larger than the tag and the design, respectively. Place the leather fuzzy side up on the StrongGrip mat and the HTV shiny side down on your LightGrip or StandardGrip mat; use a brayer to ensure they're adhered together if necessary. Depending on your mat's stickiness and the type of leather you're using, you may need to use masking tape to secure the leather to the mat; if you have a fresh mat, you shouldn't need to do this. Ensure the materials are in the same positions on the mats and on-screen – you can click and drag the images on the screen if they're not.

5 When you're happy with everything, press Continue, then follow the on-screen instructions for your leather and HTV to be cut.

6 After your machine has finished, carefully separate the materials from the cutting mats. Use your weeder tool to remove all the bits of HTV that you do not want on your luggage tag – all that should be left on your carrier sheet is your design.

7 Preheat your EasyPress Mini to its Low setting. As my tag is Cricut Genuine Leather and Cricut Heat Guide doesn't offer a recommended setting for it at the time of writing, the lowest heat setting for 30 seconds is a safe starting point to test. If you use a leather you haven't pressed before, I suggest using some scraps of it and HTV to test before pressing on your luggage tags. Place your HTV design shiny side up on your luggage tag.

8 Once your heat press has heated up, press it down on the HTV. Allow it to cool completely. Leather can be tricky, so carefully lift a corner of the carrier sheet to see if the HTV has adhered completely. If it hasn't, replace the corner of the carrier sheet and do another press over the affected area for 5 seconds. Allow it to cool again, then check it once more and repeat the press if necessary. Once the HTV is adhered in the corner, repeat this process over the rest of the tag, working on small sections at a time until all the HTV has adhered to the tag. Once you're sure all the HTV is properly adhered to the tag, slowly peel off the carrier sheet to reveal your new honeymoon accessory.

PRO TIPS:

If you're looking for a vegan-friendly alternative to leather, there are plenty of durable faux leathers and suedes that can stand up to the rigours of travel and are also Cricut-compatible. Search online for the kind you choose so you can see which blade to use.

Cricut Genuine Leather was specifically formulated for use with the deep-point blade, so it's an easy material to use. However, there are a lot of gorgeous tooling leathers out there that you may prefer to use. If you do, check the thickness to determine which blade is necessary for your project. Some leathers will be too thick for Cricut Explore and will require Cricut Maker and its knife blade.

This project's SVG can go beyond a luggage tag! Other great ideas include using the bows and titles on hats, bags, T-shirts and even shoes. And if you're attending a wedding, this SVG would make a lovely greeting card project to give to the happy couple on their big day. Your creativity is limitless!

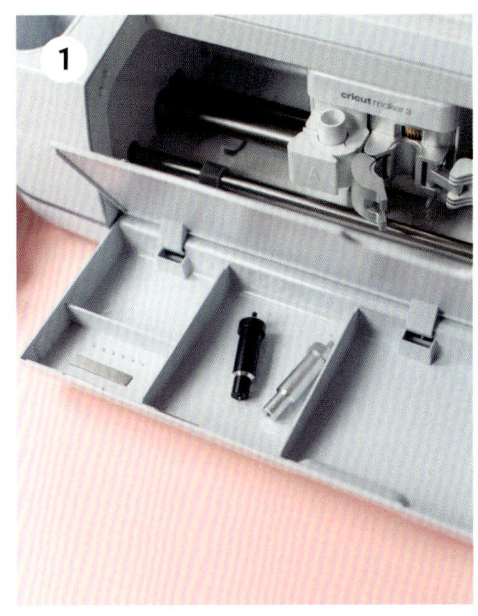
1

4
Cricut

5

5
cricut maker 3

6
Cricut

6

6

8
cricut

8
Mr &
Mr

Troubleshooting & Tips

When you only have so many DIY hours to spend and you want everything to look perfect for the big day, any snags you encounter can throw you off, but there isn't anything that's not fixable, I promise! Here are some common Cricut issues and how to fix them.

WHEN YOUR MACHINE ISN'T CUTTING PROPERLY

Whether you're working with paper for rolled flowers or vinyl for wedding party tumblers, cutting issues can happen. Here's what to investigate first:

Check Your Blade

Is it dull or dirty? Blades can wear down over time, especially when cutting thick or fibrous materials. If your cuts are dragging or not clean, look at its housing, remove the blade and give a puff of air to make sure nothing snuck inside. If it's still not right and has been used for a lot of projects, it might be time to replace the blade.

Is it the right blade for the material? Double check that you're using the correct blade – the one that Design Space prompted you to use for the type of material being cut. (You'll be surprised at how even experienced crafters sometimes forget to swap!)

Check Your Material Settings

Wrong setting selected? Ensure that your base material setting in Design Space matches what's actually on your mat. If you're using custom materials or off-brand supplies, try using the 'More' pressure option before choosing a more experimental setting.

Check Your Mat Stickiness

Is your mat well-used or not sticky enough? Materials can shift during cutting if the mat isn't clean or the tack has worn down. See page 20 for cleaning tips or try using painter's tape to hold materials in place (especially helpful for wedding projects with speciality papers like vellum). If a good wash hasn't helped, it's time for a new cutting mat.

Check the Cut Design

Is your design too intricate for the material? Thin fonts or ultra-detailed cuts may not come out well on fibrous papers or thin cardstock. Try enlarging the design, swapping the font or switching to a different material (such as vinyl) if possible. If your cardstock and fonts already pass the test, try the Intricate Cut base material setting.

Check Your Machine Calibration

For Print Then Cut or scoring heavy projects, ensure your machine is properly calibrated. You can do this under your Design Space Settings if things seem 'off' or not aligned properly. Even if you've already calibrated before, sometimes you just need to give it a go again to ensure it's currently up-to-date, especially if there have been app updates.

Contact Cricut Member Care

And last resort can be the best resort. It sounds obvious, but it sometimes escapes us to reach out to Cricut support directly! Member Care has taken care of me every time I've reached out about a problem, even helping me with a machine replacement. To make the process quicker, Cricut may ask you for details like your machine's serial number, a screenshot of your device specifications, results from an internet speed test, whether you're on a personal or work computer and even a short video showing the issue. Having these ready will help you get to a solution faster.

WHEN TRUSTED MATERIALS GO ROGUE

What happens if you experience some challenges after your machine has cut everything? While a lot can be at play with this, here are some common things I've seen and potential quick fixes:

Adhesive Vinyl

Edges lifting after a few hours or even days? It's likely that your project's surface wasn't properly cleaned before application, and therefore the vinyl didn't cure like it should have due to possible dust, oil or residue. Try removing and reapplying it after you've recleaned the surface.

Heat Transfer Vinyl

Design isn't sticking to your project after being heat pressed? It's likely that there was not enough heat, pressure or time during the heat press application. Your T-shirt or fabric blank might also have a chemical finish from its manufacturer that could make it incompatible with HTV. Try heat pressing it again. If you're using a wood blank, consider applying a fine grit sandpaper to your surface to ensure it's super smooth before trying again.

Infusible Ink

Ghosting or blurry image after heating? This happens more often than you would think! It's when the project blank or transfer sheet moves during pressing, so you get a 'shifted' look. Unfortunately, there's no quick fix for this one as you'll need to redo the project with one of your spares. For the next time, ensure everything is tightly taped down (especially where there are rounded edges) and that your heat press doesn't move while pressing. This is where the Autopress helps me most, as you'll see in the Wedding Team T-shirts project (see pages 88–91)! No shaky arthritic hands affecting my makes anymore!

WHEN YOUR WEDDING PROJECT GOES AWRY

Wedding DIY can bring its own unique challenges, but here are few tips and tricks to troubleshoot some issues you may or may not run into with Cricut projects that aren't machine-related:

Humidity and Weather

Paper curling or vinyl not sticking? If you're crafting in a humid climate or your wedding is outdoors, moisture can cause havoc with adhesives and materials, so keep your materials stored in a cool, dry place whenever possible.

Vinyl on Textured Surfaces

For wood, consider using HTV and a heat press instead of adhesive vinyl. For textured wood to be placed outdoors for a longer amount of time or in rainy conditions, seal it with a thin coat of clear water-based Polycrylic. (As an important note, sealing wedding signs isn't necessary since neither HTV or permanent adhesive vinyl on temporary installations need it.) If you choose to apply regular vinyl to textured surfaces, you can also try the old signmaker's trick and use a hair dryer over your transfer-taped vinyl, which will help it to stick better to the microscopic grooves.

Misaligned or Crooked Designs

For any design that you're having a tricky time keeping straight on your project's surface, use some washi tape as visual markers and a large ruler or T-square tool to help you line up your design. I also love to use greaseproof baking (parchment) paper underneath my vinyl designs before I attempt to put them on my blanks so I can reposition them without committing and potentially ruining my vinyl. You'll learn about this in more detail in my Wedding Welcome Mirror Sign project (see pages 100–103).

If you're doing a fabric sign, fold your fabric in half and use your EasyPress or iron to make a crease to find the middle.

If something's crooked, carefully lift the vinyl using your weeder and reposition if it hasn't fully adhered yet. For vinyl and non-porous surfaces, you can also try the wet-on-wet application method. Fill a spray bottle with some water and a drop of washing up liquid, then lightly spray it on your surface. Once your vinyl is in its correct position, use your scraper tool over the transfer tape to remove excess water. Allow to dry before removing the transfer tape.

Still a bit off? Add a small decorative element (like a mini heart or flower) to 'balance' it visually and disguise any mistakes – shh, no one will ever know!

Hard-to-Weed Design Hacks

Sometimes with white or glitter vinyl materials, it can be tricky seeing where to weed as the cut lines can look nearly invisible. I know my eyesight isn't what it used to be! For glitter materials, I do a roll-and-weed method. Because it's a thicker material, slightly bend your material where you know your design to be. The material (especially glitter HTV) should slightly lift away from the carrier sheet a bit where the cut lines are for easier weeding.

For white vinyl materials, I either use my Cricut BrightPad™ or my adjustable crafting table lamp (with a bright white LED light) at an angle so the light hits the cut lines and produces a subtle shadow for visual guidance.

Bulk Crafting Tips

Crafting in bulk for favours or signage and made mistakes on a few? Don't re-cut everything! Purchase a few extras of each blank item for emergencies. Create a 'wedding oopsie box' with back-up materials, glue dots, extra cut-outs and a weeder tool. For any paper projects, use design elements with repeatable pieces, so if one element is ruined, you can just swap it instead of redoing the whole project.

GLOSSARY

When I planned my own wedding in the UK, I quickly discovered just how many wedding words didn't quite translate across the Atlantic. As someone who grew up with 'cocktail hours' and 'rehearsal dinners', I was baffled when I first heard words like 'wedding breakfast' and 'drinks reception'. (Spoiler: no pancakes involved, and rehearsal dinners don't exist here!)

Since this book is written in British English but my heart belongs to both sides of the pond, I thought a little glossary would be helpful to all readers. If nothing else, consider it fun wedding facts! Think of it as a bridge between my two worlds — a lighthearted guide to make sure no matter where you're celebrating, you will know exactly what's what throughout this book.

- Bachelor Party (US) – Stag Do (UK) – Pre-wedding celebration for the groom and close friends.
- Bachelorette Party (US) – Hen Do (UK) – Pre-wedding celebration for the bride and close friends.
- Boutonniere (US) – Buttonhole (UK) – Small floral arrangement worn on a suit's lapel.
- Cocktail Hour (US) – Drinks Reception (UK) – Post-ceremony event before dinner for snacks, drinks and mingling among the guests.
- Engagement Photos (US) – Pre-Wedding Photoshoot (UK) – Professional photos of the couple before the wedding day.
- Hors d'oeuvres/Appetizers (US) – Canapés (UK) – Small bites served at cocktail hour/reception.
- Head Table (US) – Top Table (UK) – The main table where the couple and close family sit.
- Maid/Matron of Honor (US) – Chief Bridesmaid (UK) – Bride's main attendant.
- Officiant (US) – Registrar/Vicar/Celebrant (UK) – Person legally or ceremonially marrying the couple.
- Rehearsal Dinner (US) – None (UK) – US tradition of a meal with family and wedding party after a ceremony run-through; UK rehearsals aren't common.
- Registry (US) – Gift List (UK) – Where guests can select gifts for the couple.
- Seating Chart (US) – Table Plan (UK) – How guests find where they are seated at dinner.
- Timeline (US) – Order of the Day (UK) – Same meaning of what's happening on the wedding day.
- Tuxedo (US) – Morning Suit (UK) – Both formalwear, but each serve a different attire purpose. The UK views tuxedos strictly as evening wear, not for daytime weddings.
- Vendor (US) – Supplier (UK) – Person or company providing wedding goods/services.
- Venue Coordinator (US) – Events Manager (UK) – Staff member overseeing wedding day details for the venue.
- Wedding Reception (US) – Wedding Breakfast (UK) – Final event of the wedding day with dinner and entertainment.

Popular Cricut Wedding Questions

Based on enquiries from Tidewater and Tulle, reading through real posts by brides, grooms and soonlyweds in social media community groups, and from my own in-person workshops, these six questions are some that pop up over and over again. And with good reason! If you're completely new to Cricut, you've just entered a whole shiny world of creative possibility and that comes with curiosity.

Do I Need the Most Expensive Cricut Machine for Wedding Projects?

No! I've learned a lot of first-time Cricut users actually get a Cricut machine because of their weddings, and a good chunk of those people get theirs second-hand or receive one as a gift. Everyone's story is different, so 'expensive' is subjective. Couples who fall in love with the idea of creating things for their weddings tend to not want limitations on what they can make, so Cricut Maker family is considered a favourite as it can cut more materials due to its rotary blade and knife blade. But for those who know exactly what they want to create and love thinking outside the box, they may find that any of the Cricut machines can meet their needs.

How Much Should I Estimate for My Cricut Wedding Projects?

It sounds like a funny answer, but that depends on you and your wedding vision! You will need a cutting machine, blades, materials and perhaps other craft supplies. Some may get a second-hand machine, some may prefer a brand-new one. Some may already have craft supplies, some may not. Some are having an intimate wedding with 25 guests, and some with 200 or more. The best way to budget for your DIY projects is to look at your personal wedding needs and your guest count. Set a budget and then work within that budget as cleverly as you can. You would be amazed at what you can find when you start asking your loved ones for advice and other DIY couples online, too!

Can I Make a Whole Wedding With Just a Cricut Joy?

It depends. If you are doing primarily simple small-scaled projects, absolutely! But for anything that is wider than 4.25in (11cm), you might struggle to get the results you want. If you get really clever, you'll eventually learn ways to break up large projects into sections that can then be cut on a Joy machine, but it's not an effortless, new beginner-friendly task, can be time-consuming and is potentially costly. Cricut Joy is a small but mighty machine, and still a lot of wedding projects can be done with it as you'll see in this book's projects, but it is ultimately limited in size and what it can do compared to the rest of the Cricut machines out there.

Where Can I Find Wedding Fonts or SVGs That Don't Look 'Everyday'?

As a fellow font nerd, I get it. Fonts are everything when it comes to design! It makes or breaks a project. Not all fonts perform the same when cutting on a machine, particularly the beautiful wedding-perfect script or cursive ones that have varied line thicknesses. This was asked so much that I had to write an article about it, and it's a frequently visited one! Go to www.tidewaterandtulle.com and search for 'cricut font' if you want to read a more in-depth article on this.

Will Vinyl Stick to Glass/Wood/Fabric/ Whatever for the Whole Wedding Day?

Adhesive vinyl comes with its own sticky adhesive backing, so this can be readily applied to most any surface. See page 34 for more information on vinyl types. Heat transfer vinyl is more suited for wood and fabric applications and needs a heat press to activate its adhesion. When you use the correct type of vinyl for your surface, it will absolutely last far beyond the wedding day!

What's the Easiest Cricut Wedding Project for Total Beginners?

All of the projects in this book have been designed for beginners to both Cricut and crafting. Start with a simple vinyl project like Photo Frame Table Numbers (see pages 120–123) – it's great for getting a feel of how things are made with a Cricut machine and how to work with a material. By the time you finish reading this book, you should be well on your way to becoming more confident in creating magical things!

Sourcing Wedding Supplies

As much as I live and breathe weddings, I know first-hand how overwhelming the planning can be, especially when it comes to all the stuff involved in creating a meaningful event. From personalized signage to custom favours, the list adds up fast. And, unfortunately, many of these single-use details can end up as physical and financial waste after the big day, much to your dismay after the confetti settles. That's why I want to be intentional in how I guide you through sourcing your wedding craft supplies – not just where to find them, but how to choose them in a way that aligns with your values, budget and wedding style.

Before diving into the where, let's take a moment to think about the why behind each DIY project you are hoping to create. What matters most to you?

- On a smaller budget? Start by deciding which DIY details are must-haves.
- Eco-conscious? Look into materials that are sustainable or reusable.
- Planning a destination wedding? Consider what's travel-friendly or can be shipped in advance.
- Want to support small businesses? See if local or indie shops carry what you need.

So how exactly am I defining 'wedding craft supplies'? Beyond Cricut-specific materials, these are items like fabric, ribbon, paint, dried flowers, wooden signs, glass vases, glue, easels and decorative paper. They are essentially anything that you would use to make or finish your wedding DIY.

You should also become familiar with the term 'blank' – your plain, undecorated project surface. These are the items you will customize such as pre-cut acrylic sheets, fabric banners, wood slices, photo frames, denim jackets . . . and the list goes on. If it's blank, it's ready for your creative touch!

For this book, I've used genuine Cricut products wherever relevant – not only because I've been a longtime fan (hello, emotionally invested here!), but also because they're beginner-friendly and widely available in the countries where this book is sold. That said, all of this is inspirational to help you decide what works for you, your budget, your craft confidence level and personal preferences.

Each project in this book was created with flexibility and accessibility in mind. Many of the supplies I used were sourced from my own craft stash, online second-hand marketplaces, small female-founded businesses or eco-minded brands that align with my own values. And for transparency, I did have some support from Cricut UK for the Cricut materials in this book since there was a lot of prototyping, testing and creating involved to ensure everything in reality is perfect for your crafting experience.

Every project has also been designed so that you can recreate it with similar supplies no matter where you live – and often in bulk, perfect for weddings, big or small. So let's get right to it: on the following pages you'll find my insight on where to find the craft supplies that'll help bring your wedding vision to life.

Direct

Sometimes direct is best for a diverse array of options. This is the case with finding supplies to use with your Cricut machine. If you're looking for a certain colour cardstock or genuine blades, Cricut's website is a great place to start looking to see the range and what types of deals are available. Cricut inventory may vary depending on your country, so researching in advance is a good idea.

Many couples also find off-brand vinyls and heat transfer vinyls perfect for their crafting as some colours are not available in on-brand materials. Ordering from these other suppliers directly may also save some money as suppliers may pay a fee to be on large online marketplaces, so they are happy to pass on the savings via their own retail website.

Chain & Online Retailers

Depending on where you're located, large physical retailers can be your quickest option. Because of their established presence, these brick-and-mortar shops tend to have coupons, sales and loyalty programmes that can sometimes help you get inspired and stay within your budget. Hobbycraft (UK) and Michaels (North America) are just some of the leading arts and crafts shops that carry Cricut products as well as other craft supplies, so you might be able to get everything you need in one visit.

Amazon's vast product variety and accessibility into remote communities appeals to many first-time crafters, while IKEA is also a fast-favourite resource for wedding couples everywhere as their product style is minimalist, making their items perfect for wedding DIY blank personalization. From wooden crates transformed into autumn wedding blanket boxes to tabletop greenhouses into card boxes, the ideas really are endless.

Discount shops also provide loads of home decor blanks that could be transformed into wedding decor with some vinyl treatment. It's where I found the mirror for my Wedding Welcome Mirror Sign project (see pages 100–103). A lot of my DIY tutorials on Tidewater and Tulle mention supplies or blanks from bargain shops. You'd never know they're budget by looking – it's all in the styling and training your eye to see beauty everywhere.

Pre-loved Shops

Whether you call them thrift stores or charity shops, these can be gold mines for wedding craft supplies! From blank vases to ribbons to, yes, even Cricut machines, it's a bit of a treasure hunt every time. I don't recommend relying fully on these stores to find everything you need, especially if you're restricted on time or want a specific type of product, but they are wonderful sources to find bulk project blanks and random craft treasures.

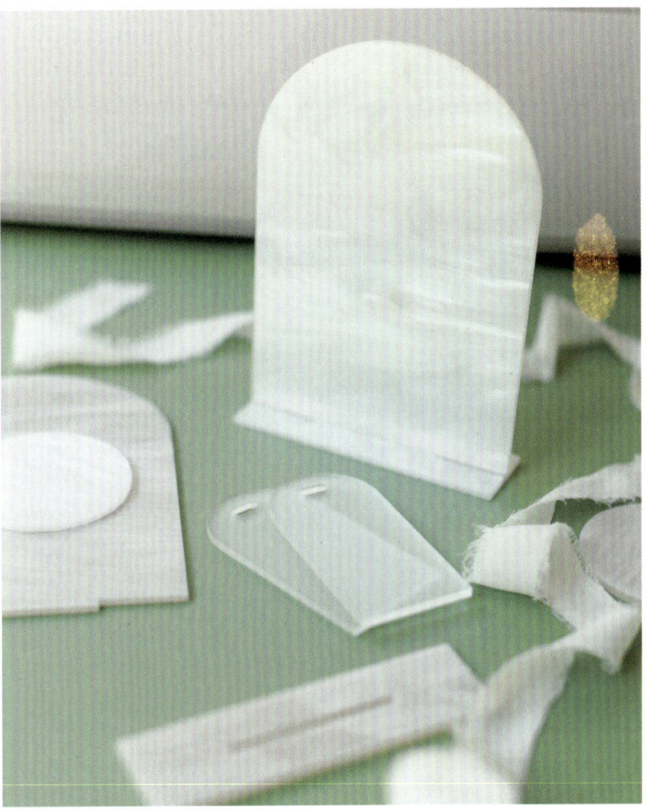

I found most of my own small wedding's outdoor reception throw blankets at charity shops – it took me four months of constantly looking to get my 12 grey blankets, but I did it! (They now have been lovingly adopted by our cats and are living their best upcycled life.)

Some communities also have non-profit craft-dedicated scrap shops or donation-driven home improvement stores. Search online to see if your local area has one. They're sometimes called recycled arts and crafts, but mostly they are supported by local crafters donating new and gently used craft supplies, so you can then purchase to support local efforts and eco-friendly practices. It can be a great place to find fabric remnants, yarn, embroidery thread, beads, paper and other miscellaneous craft supplies.

Online Second-Hand Marketplaces & Community Groups

We don't always have immediate access to the brick-and-mortar stores, especially if you live in smaller rural towns, and that's where online communities come in to fill the gaps. You can find oodles of past wedding couples selling their pre-loved or excess wedding supplies in social media groups – most commonly called 'Wedding Sell and Buy' groups. Sometimes these are local, sometimes they're further away, but always a great place to find a bargain.

If you don't use social media, online second-hand marketplaces such as eBay and Vinted may offer more buyer confidence and better search options for specific products. You can find a lot of second-hand Cricut-specific products on these platforms as well as blanks like shoes, jackets, acrylic shapes and sign easels that you can create with.

Around Your Home

Have you poked around your home yet to see what could be transformed by your Cricut machine? Not only is this one of the best free 'hacks' but it means the thing you're using may go back to your home after the big day as well! Ask your friends and family if they are decluttering their homes or have anything on your supply list. You may be helping them check something off of their own chore list! Home-sourced blanks can be especially great for personalizing and upcycling clothing, vases, mirrors, picture frames and more.

Acknowledgements

'There is nothing I would not do for those who are really my friends. I have no notion of loving people by halves, it is not my nature.' – Jane Austen

To Mr B, thank you for being my number one cheerleader. There still isn't a day that goes by that I don't count my lucky stars that our souls found each other again in this lifetime. You not only embrace, but unwaveringly encourage my lofty creative visions and purpose-driven passion in everything I do. I love you with the intensity of a thousand cats loudly staring down an open tuna tin.

To Damaris, Liss, Tyler, Jenn and Emily — thank you for always keeping it weird, loving me through every chapter (literal and emotional) and checking in when I needed it most. This book carries your laughter and encouragement on every page.

To all my loved ones — near and far — who have supported this journey (and being all prophetic, telling me I was going to write a book decades ago) with your kind words and bottomless funny reels. They have been cherished. Consider this the biggest bookish hug!

To Cat Madeira — I literally couldn't have done it without you! You were so gracious with my ADHD brain when taking my (really rough) design ideas and digitizing them into gorgeous SVGs, and consequently all the edits I asked of you. Dream collaboration! Obrigada, my friend!

To Jessica Bishop, Cori George and Paula Milner, thank you for answering all of my non-fiction author/book publishing questions and sharing your experiences from already having 'been there, done that.' Your insight was appreciated and gave me the boost to 'say yes' to this whole journey!

To my fellow Cricut UK Ambassadors, thank you for warmly and enthusiastically welcoming me into the group without hesitation. You knew how hard immigration was for me, and you made me feel like a genuine part of a community instantly. Extra thanks to Oriana and Soph for cheer check-ins, Caz for all the borrows and Samara for topper help!

To Tom, Robin, Ellie, all of the Jonathans and the GMC staff, there is so much gratitude that you've let me run wild with this one, especially as your first wedding niche book! Thank you for truly being a supportive publishing partner from day one. I'm one lucky gal!

To every single Tidewater and Tulle reader, sponsor and friend over the years: you gave me hope to keep going in a mercurial digital publication world with the ever-changing algorithms. Thank you for believing in the power of heartfelt love stories and in the beauty of personalized weddings. Here's to many more years ahead.

Partners & Friends

GMC Publications and Chelsea would like to express their utmost gratitude to Cricut UK for providing a lot of the materials and general support used in this book. While this book is not sponsored, endorsed or associated with Cricut in any way, the help from Kathy Hodson, Kate Smith, Fi Thomas and Nic Walker was beyond appreciated.

Our thanks also go to our wonderful partners for their own contribution and services in making this book happen:

SVG Creation: Cat Madeira
Photo Shoot Assistant: Robert Barton
Photo Shoot Planning Assistance: Kelsie Scully Photography
Venue: Buxted Park Hotel
Florals: The Floral Hire
Styling: Ambience Venue Styling Kent West
Wedding Content Creation: Han Picked Memories
Make-up: Leanna Codd Makeup
Hair: Hair By Eloise
Bride's Attire: BRIDE By Aster
Bridesmaid Attire: TH&TH Bridesmaids
Catering: Rose Petal Cake Company
Mobile Bar: Southdowns Bar Co.
Cake: Bubba's Bakes
Models: Nishaa Sharma-Salter and Chloe Eells

Together is a beautiful place to be.
MARINA & ALASTAIR

Further Resources

CRICUT EDUCATION

Angie Holden: www.thecountrychiccottage.net
Craft with Sarah: www.craftwithsarah.com
Hey, Let's Make Stuff!: www.heyletsmakestuff.com
Jennifer Maker: www.jennifermaker.com
The Cricut Club: www.thecricutclub.com
Tidewater and Tulle: www.tidewaterandtulle.com

CRICUT & CRAFT SUPPLIES

You will find a clickable supply list for every project on www.cricutweddings.com

Global

Cricut: www.cricut.com

USA

Amazon: www.amazon.com
American Crafts (cardstock): www.americancrafts.com
Michaels: www.michaels.com, www.michaels.ca
Paper Source: www.papersource.com

UK

Amazon: www.amazon.co.uk
Eco Craft: www.eco-craft.co.uk
Fred Aldous: www.fredaldous.co.uk
Hobbycraft: www.hobbycraft.co.uk
John Lewis: www.johnlewis.com
Søstrene Grene: www.sostrenegrene.com
The Range: www.therange.co.uk

SVG FILES

Cat Madeira: www.catmadeira.com
Design Pixie: www.designpixie.com
Dinosaur Mama: www.dinosaurmama.com
Tidewater and Tulle: www.tidewaterandtulle.com

WEDDING DIY BLANKS & SUPPLIES

Global

Etsy: www.etsy.com
Vinted: www.vinted.com

USA

Afloral: www.afloral.com
Dollar Tree: www.dollartree.com
IKEA: www.ikea.com
Ling's Moment: www.lingsmoment.com
Vinted: www.vinted.com
World Market: www.worldmarket.com

UK

Dunelm: www.dunelm.com
Ginger Ray: www.gingerray.co.uk
IKEA: www.ikea.co.uk
Poundland: www.poundland.co.uk
Vinted: www.vinted.co.uk

SVG FILES FOR THIS BOOK

Download the SVG files for the projects in this book using this QR code and the password CWGMC1111

About the Author

Chelsea Barton is a leading voice in wedding DIY. A former wedding photographer and the founder of Tidewater and Tulle, she's spent over 17 years helping couples bring their dream weddings to life through creative, approachable ideas.

Building on that passion, Chelsea has been designing wedding DIY tutorial content for Cricut and other international lifestyle brands since 2016 with no end of the aisle in sight. When she's not wearing her editorial hat, she freelances as a Cricut UK Ambassador, leading in-store demonstrations at Hobbycraft, John Lewis and other British retailers, as well as teaching her own artful craft workshops.

Her insight and work have been featured in *Martha Stewart Weddings*, *Southern Living*, *Hello! Middle East*, *SheKnows* and other top publications around the world. With a passion for beautiful, meaningful celebrations, she blends editorial expertise with hands-on craft knowledge to inspire brides, grooms and soonlyweds everywhere.

Originally from Virginia, Chelsea now resides in southern England with her British husband, affectionately known as Mr B, and their two cats, Miss Pickles Barrington and Juniper McIntyre.

Connect with Chelsea on social media at @cricutweddings, @makewithchelsea, and @tidewatertulle for even more wedding DIY and lifestyle inspiration. You can also find her and her other wedding projects that you can make on Cricut Design Space under the profile name 'Make with Chelsea'.

www.cricutweddings.com
www.makewithchelsea.com
www.tidewaterandtulle.com

Index

First published 2026 by
Guild of Master Craftsman Publications Ltd,
Castle Place, 166 High Street, Lewes, East Sussex,
BN7 1XU, UK
www.gmcbooks.com

ISBN 978 1 78494 724 8

The EEA authorised representative is
Authorised Rep Compliance Ltd.
Ground Floor, 71 Baggot Street Lower,
Dublin, DO2 P593, Ireland
www.arccompliance.com

A catalogue record for this book is available from the British Library.

Publisher Jonathan Bailey
Production Director Jim Bulley
Design Manager Robin Shields
Senior Project Editor Tom Kitch
Designer Ellie Smith
Editor Theresa Bebbington

Colour origination by GMC Reprographics
Printed and bound in China

To order a book, contact:
GMC Publications Ltd
Castle Place, 166 High Street,
Lewes, East Sussex, BN7 1XU,
United Kingdom
Tel: +44 (0)1273 488005
www.gmcbooks.com

THE GUILD OF MASTER CRAFTSMAN
PUBLICATIONS